THE 'CITY' CENTENARY

1891–1991

by

JOHN SLEIGHT

A history of the City of Newcastle Golf Club,
one of the premier clubs in the North of England.

First published in 1991
by the City of Newcastle Golf Club Ltd.
Three Mile Bridge, Gosforth, Newcastle upon Tyne.

Design and Illustrations: Alan Lambert, Wideopen, Newcastle upon Tyne.
Photography: Alan Proudlock, Kenton Park Centre, Newcastle upon Tyne.

ISBN 0–9517454–0–9

Printed by Hindson Print Ltd, Newcastle upon Tyne

J. Beaumont Pease, first Club Champion of the City of Newcastle G.C. and inaugural winner of the Northumberland County Championship in 1907. An English International, he was Captain of the Royal and Ancient Club of St. Andrews in 1931. Later, he was elevated to the peerage for his services to banking, taking the title of Lord Wardington.

Left: Maurice Beck, Past President and Centenary Year Captain.

Right: Brian Goldwater, Past Captain and Centenary Year President.

Contents

		Page
	List of Illustrations	vi
	Introduction	vii
Chapter I	The 'City G.C.' is Born	1
Chapter II	The Testing Years: 1891–1907	9
Chapter III	Arrival at the Three Mile Bridge – 1907 (First Card of the Course; The Stymie; Newcastle United G.C.)	17
Chapter IV	Douglas Edgar – Great Golfer of His Time. Dr. Alister Mackenzie – Course Architect of Repute	25
Chapter V	Twenty-five Busy Years, 1914–1939	39
Chapter VI	Trials of World War II and the Post War Years	45
Chapter VII	The Golf Explosion ('City G.C.' League Champions; Holes in 1 Record; and Scots Wha Hae!)	49
Chapter VIII	The Trophies – Club and County	53
Chapter IX	The David Moffat Story	57
Chapter X	'City G.C.' Forges Ahead.	
	Major Development Schemes	65
	Jottings from the 1970's and 1980's	66
	Into the 1990's	72
Chapter XI	Portraits of Some Fine 'City' Players	83
Chapter XII	The Great Golfing Marathon	93
Chapter XIII	Some Club Characters	95
Chapter XIV	The Ladies at the 'City G.C.'	105
Chapter XV	The Juniors	117
Chapter XVI	The 'City' Professionals	121
Chapter XVII	The Seniors	127
	Acknowledgements and Thanks	128
Appendix	Captains, Presidents, Club Champions and Club Honours	129

List of Illustrations

	Page
J. Beaumont Pease, first County Champion and first Club Champion	iii
Centenary Captain and President	iv
The Windmill, first Headquarters	x
First score-card, Three Mile Bridge	22–23
Douglas Edgar portrait	24
Edgar introduces the modern golf swing; and on the tee at 'The Park'	29
First President opens Town Moor Course. Original petition to Freemen	30
Signators shown in original petition. John Boyd, Past Capt., Hon. Solicitor	31
Early makes of golf balls. Wood made in 1890's by first Professional	32
A Captain of 'The City' in 1914. Crow killed at opening of new course	33
Two views of the old windmill clubhouse	34
Original clubhouse at Three Mile Bridge. Early plan of course lay-out	35
Captain's drive-in 1934. A golfing group of members in 1930's	36
A 1950's cartoon of Northumberland Championship: Moffat v Dunn	37
Joe Harvey, once a regular player at 'The City'. Cartoon of 1970's	38
Cromer Moffat plays 'The Stymie' in inter-county event of late 1920's	44
'Tot' Colpitts, loyal servant and great character	47
A quartet of 'City' stalwarts	48
The Club's Trophies. Group of Past Captains	54
Two Northumberland Championship victories by David Moffat	58
Moffat v Clark in 1956 Final. Moffat drives off to victory in 1969	59
Moffat pictured in Centenary Year	62
Newcastle and District League Squad 1991. The Club Committee 1990/91	73
Rare photograph of special Championship Final for 'City G.C.'	74
A quartet of Triple 'City' winners 1946/47	74
Two members who featured in the 'Great Golfing Marathon'	75
John Duncan driving off the first tee in his Captain's year	75
The one and only Stan Quine. Captain's Day snap-shots 1977	76
Two Past Captains who gave great service to the club	77
Ben Clark – making local golfing history	78
Card of present course record set by Michael Blackburn	79
Trophy night 1990	80–81
Ernie Sullivan – scratch player	82
More Triple Winners of County Trophies. A County Team that made history	89
Cartoon of two early 'City' characters	104
Shirley Beck, Centenary Year Lady Captain	112
First Minute Book of 'Three Mile Bridge Ladies' Golf Club'	112
Lady President 1990–91. A mother-daughter partnership in county victory	113
Northumberland Ladies – All-England Champions. A powerful ladies quartet	114
Ladies' League Teams of 1991	115
The Ladies Committee of 1990–91. A Ladies Captain's Day group of 1985	116
First Northumberland Junior League Squad. The Junior League Team 1991	118
Anthony Matthew, Club Professional	120
Sam McRae, the longest serving Professional	122
Northumberland Senior League Squad 1991	126

Introduction

THE ROYAL AND ANCIENT GAME AND THE 'CITY G.C.'

The rich history of the City of Newcastle Golf Club reveals links with three of the master golfers of a 100 years ago. Two of them became famous – Tom Morris Senior and Harry Vardon – winners of the Open Championship ten times between them.

The third I call 'The Unknown Genius'. For, although Douglas Edgar of Newcastle upon Tyne was one of the best golfers of his era, winning several Open Championships in different countries, his name has slipped almost into oblivion.

This book attempts to redress this oversight, and tell this 'Geordie's' compelling story of international golf success, which included a victory over the great Bobby Jones.

In writing a history which begins a century ago, the author is tempted to examine the origins of golf in order to put into perspective the birth date of one's particular club. This author is no exception, and looking at the extended history of golf, the first surprise is to discover how long it took for club golf to come to an important centre like Newcastle upon Tyne. There is documentary proof that golf was being played in and around Edinburgh as long ago as the 1400's; it took some 400 years to move south of the border to Tyneside.

The explanation is that in England, for various reasons, golf is a comparatively recent phenomenon; many English clubs were only founded around the turn of the century.

Founded on October 1st, 1891 the 'City G.C.' was the first club to be formed on the Town Moor (though a form of golf was played by individuals on a limited number of holes before that).

Early golfers on the Town Moor appeared after the Newcastle Corporation and the Freemen laid out 35 acres as a recreation ground in 1880. Football, cricket and bowling were the major pastimes, and the germ of golf had only an ephemeral existence, receiving little sympathy from the authorities.

Even the oldest club in Northumberland, Alnmouth, was not founded until 1869, though it is known that individuals were playing on the coastal links before the club was formed.

The only explanation for the tardy arrival of golf in these parts was that at the end of the 19th century, the game was one for the well-to-do. The pre-requisities were leisure time, transport, and money to purchase clubs and balls and to hire caddies on the course.

The class that could afford all of those things were people of noble birth and merchants and businessmen of means. There were hardly any golf clubs in the country at the start of the 19th century, though by its end there were well over 2,000.

Modern golf really began in the early 1900's with the invention of the Haskell Ball (Coburn Haskell, an American patented the first core-wound ball in 1899, producing extra length and resilience). Later, the game received added momentum with the introduction of the first steel shafts.

If one can trace the explosion of modern golf with some certainty, it is a more difficult task trying to trace the origins of the game itself. No one knows for certain who actually invented the game of golf. Various countries lay claim to the origination of the game, including France and Belgium. Though both the Scots and the Dutch claim to have fathered the game as it is played today. The Scottish claim appears to be the more substantial with the harder evidence. As early as 1457, Royal Statutes signed by James IV prohibited the game of golf 'lest it should interfere with the more important accomplishment of archery'.

The Italians reckon that their Roman ancestors introduced golf to Britain and the Low Countries. The Dutch possess antique prints showing a game played long ago called 'Kolf' or 'Kolven' using curved sticks, a small ball and a hole as a target. Some sources claim that a form of the game was being played in England in the 14th century when it was called 'Cambuca'.

The earliest documentary proof of golf being played in Newcastle upon Tyne is an archive showing that King Charles I in 1646 played several rounds of golf on the Shield Field when he was held captive by the Scottish invaders. That appears to be an isolated example; there is no further sound evidence of the game being played in Newcastle until the closing decades of the 19th century.

If there is uncertainty about the origins of the game, one can positively state that St. Andrews is acknowledged as the 'Cradle of Golf' in modern times. In Scotland, the first rules were laid down and the first organised clubs – the Royal Burgess Golf Society and the Hon. Company of Edinburgh Golfers – were formed. Thereafter, St. Andrews became the headquarters of the game; the home of the Patriarch of Golf, Tom Morris; and the location for the organising body of the world of golf – the Royal and Ancient Club.

The City of Newcastle is fortunate to possess such strong links with the 'Father' of the game, old Tom Morris. He won the 'Open Championship' four times, and occasionally competed in Northern England including an annual tournament at Alnmouth.

He was approaching 70 when he laid out the first 'City' golf course on the Town Moor; records show that he was favourably impressed with this huge green carpet so close to the city and covering more than 1,200 acres of attractive moorland.

If one considers the spread of the game abroad, it was mostly due to Scottish professionals taking up residence in North America that the game took off in the United States. Although there were one or two Englishmen who emigrated to America to take up professional appointments at golf clubs.

One of those was a good-looking, outstanding player called Douglas Edgar who started his life as a 'Pro' with the post of Assistant to J. S. Caird, the 'City' Professional on the Town Moor in the 1890's. Later Edgar was the 'Pro' at the Northumberland Club before departing for Atlanta, Georgia. There is documentary evidence which states that Douglas Edgar was one of a band of British Pro's who taught the Americans the modern golf swing. He became known for the art of his tuition and his thinking about the fundamentals of the golf swing.

His book on how to play the game, called 'The Gate to Golf' was said by that master golfer, Tommy Armour, to be the best there was. (Armour didn't write a bad book himself. 'How to Play Your Best Golf All the Time' became a best-seller, if not 'The Bible' of golf instruction.)

In our centenary year, we pay homage to the Royal and Ancient Club, formed in 1754 and given the Royal Accolade in 1834, for bestowing its wisdom and rulings on this complicated game for so long without serious challenge. When they confirmed our founding date as October, 1891, (a different date had been mistakingly held by the Club in earlier years) they also informed us that two other clubs also celebrate their centenaries this year: Warkworth G.C. (September 1891) and Rothbury (December 1891). Congratulations to both!

At this time, our thoughts go back to the men of vision who made the City of Newcastle G.C. a reality a 100 years ago.

We, the members, will never cease to be in their debt.

The birthplace of the City of Newcastle Golf Club. This attractive five-sail windmill built in 1782, known as Chimney Mill, was the novel headquarters of the Club from 1891–1907. Photograph taken from rear but note lovely windows and top of a solarium (left) which afforded commanding views over the Town Moor course.

Chapter I

THE 'CITY' IS BORN

When the City of Newcastle Golf Club was founded in October, 1891, Victoria, Queen of Great Britain, Empress of India and Ruler of the mighty British Empire had 10 more years to reign; the Olympic Games – lying dormant – were about to be revived; and Tom Morris Senior, four times Open Champion and the patriarch of British golf had completed his lay-out for the first 'City' course on Newcastle's Town Moor, remarking, 'This could become one of the finest inland courses in the country'.

As it transpired, the Club was in for a short stay on the Moor, a mere 16 years before circumstances forced a move to present headquarters at the Three Mile Bridge. This has been a happy home now for more than 80 years. It says much for the managers of the day that another golfing great, Harry Vardon, six times Open Champion and a member of the 'Great Triumverate' of Taylor, Braid and Vardon who dominated British golf for many years before World War I, was engaged to design the present course.

The centenary of any golf club is a glorious landmark. In celebrating 100 years of golf, thoughts should go back to that small band of 'City' pioneers who started it all by moving into a lovely 18th-century windmill on the edge of the Town Moor, and converting it to become the first clubhouse and H.Q. of the City of Newcastle G.C.

Throughout the years, the name of the City of Newcastle G.C. has been linked with many honours including English internationals and county championships.

But to assume that the life of the 'City' has been plain-sailing over the century would be a misnomer. On several occasions, financial crises shook the 'City' to its foundations; at one point, permanent closure looked a distinct possibility, and at another crisis point the 'City' did actually close for three months in order to raise money by reaping in the harvest from the Grange Farm site.

The 'City' ship undoubtedly sailed through some very rough waters – through the turbulent times of two world wars, and the great unrest and bitterness of the General Strike in the 1920's. Somehow, the 'City' ship never actually foundered in any of the storms, though drastic action on more than one occasion saved the day.

By the late 1950's, and with two world wars behind them allowing them to build up membership, the future looked rather rosy. Although the Club was always conscious of the fact that they did not own the land that they played on.

A devastating blow in 1958 came in the form of a letter from the landlords who informed the 'City G.C.' that they were to commandeer a large area of their land, and our golf course, to the South. The land was urgently needed by the local Education Committee.

'City' members were horrified to learn that holes No. 2 to No. 8 would be lost, a section of the course which then ran alongside the Broadway.

The 'City G.C.' managers turned a possible disaster into something of a triumph. They met the challenge head-on, and saw that the solution was to extend the lay-out to the West which would enable them to lengthen the course and introduce several new features. By 1960 the necessary new trees and greens were laid out on former farm-land which was well suited to the purpose.

So that when the 'City' golfers played the new course for the first time in 1963, they found holes re-numbered and the length extended from 6,241 yards to 6,602 yards. The longer course now produced a new, demanding challenge; and although the effect of the re-construction was applauded, there were some members who complained about the new course favouring the big hitters and the low handicap men. In time, the moans died away, so that the 'City' today presents a fair, but tough scoring proposition off the tiger-tees.

Looking back over the years, we are proud of our history at the City of Newcastle. And although we were the first golf club to be established within the precincts of Newcastle City, we cannot lay claim to playing the game as far back as the 17th century.

It was King Charles I who, in 1646 played rounds of golf on the old Shield Field outside the city walls. Although he was held by Scottish invaders who had successfully laid siege to the town, he was allowed to fill the hours of the day by playing a favourite pastime. It was at least another two centuries before the golf game became available to the commoners; and it took some time to take hold in Northumberland and Newcastle even though the game was being played in Scotland many years before the 'City G.C.' opened.

Locally, the City of Newcastle Club can lay claim to association with the beginnings of two other clubs. When the United Workmens' Club artisan group of golfers formed in 1892, they came to agreement with the 'City G.C.' to play the new Town Moor course, and shared the services of the 'City G.C.' Professional. The 'City G.C.' paid the clubhouse rent and all maintenance and running expenses connected with the course. The arrangement seemed to run smoothly, and old records show that matches between the 'City' and 'United' were held from time to time.

The 'City G.C.' has strong links too, with the beginnings of the Northumberland Club at Gosforth Park. By 1898, a considerable number of 'City G.C.' members became disenchanted with life on the Town Moor. Its open public space attracted 'golfers' who were members of neither the 'City' nor 'United', and whose encroachment was a continuing source of irritation. As a result, a group of 'City G.C.' golfers broke away and contributed to the foundation of the Northumberland Golf Club. Records show that later one member of 'The Park', Joseph Miller, a chartered accountant, a great character and fine golfer linked himself to the 'City' by presenting the Joseph Miller Salver in 1934 for annual competition.

The history of the 'City' Golf Club is bursting with golden memories of outstanding matches won and lost; of records set and holes in 1 won; of outstanding characters and active workers for the club. But how did the 'City' come to be formed and who was responsible for its birth? Before beginning the story of the pregnancy and birth of the 'City G.C.', consider for a moment golfing happenings in the area in the preceding years. From about 1850 the Town Moor, known then as 'The Freemen's Preserves' was much used for sporting pursuits. The 'Newcastle Daily Journal' records that up to the turn of the century, some of the favourite pastimes were football, cricket and two popular forms of bowls – 'pot-shares' and 'houging' – which were so physical they had to be played along a measured track. Some people played a form of golf on the Recreation Ground laid out in 1880 though there was no club formed.

The fact was that these early golfers met with little sympathy from the Town Moor authorities, and the germ of golf had only an ephemeral existence. A number of clubs had been formed in the area, prior to the foundation of the 'City' Club. Alnmouth was the oldest, born in 1869 with Earl Percy as the first Captain and the Duke of Northumberland first President. Later, other clubs were formed including Berwick-upon-Tweed, Tyneside, Seaton Carew, Newbiggin, Whitley Bay, Hexham and Bamburgh. So with much golf activity going on around them, it was not surprising that a number of Newcastle men should come together with the intention of forming their own club.

Early in 1891 in the drawing room of a large Jesmond house, a small group of Newcastle professional and businessmen met to discuss the possibility of forming a golf club in the city. They deliberated well into the night, but at the end of that inaugural meeting the blue-print for the founding of the City of Newcastle Golf Club had been drawn up. The pioneers had decided that the Town Moor would suitably convert into a good golf course; so they drew up a petition to present to the authorities who governed the Moor.

This small band of enthusiasts was not unaware that there would be difficulties ahead. They could anticipate opposition to the playing of a rather 'aristocratic' sport on an attractive open moor which was a public place so close to the city itself; a place where the populace turned for their outdoor pastimes.

Even so, the petitioners must have been somewhat shocked by the depth of opposition in the City Council Chamber.

The fact was that the 'City G.C.' pioneers had to negotiate and deal with two different authorities: the Corporation who held the freehold of the land, and the Freemen who held the freehold of the herbiage by an Act of Parliament of 1774.

The public rights of the Town Moor – with a history going back some 2,000 years – were jealously guarded. Other complications included the statutory rights of the Freemen of Newcastle. Every Freeman had the official right to graze two cows each on the Moor for as long as he desired; so a newly laid-out golf course would have to take into account the presence of cattle on the links.

The pioneers, who pressed ahead against all odds, were:

Dr. Adam Wilson, a medical practitioner
John R. Bolton
J. M. Redmayne, a Mosley St. businessman
F. Kaye
John Turnbull
Dr. J. B. Black, medical practitioner

The petition also had the full backing of a leading Newcastle citizen living at Pendower, J. W. Pease – a name that would play a major role in the history of the City of Newcastle Golf Club in the years to come. . . .

The petition to the Freemen stated:

'We, the under-signed, acknowledging the rights of the Freemen of this city over the pasturage on the Town Moor beg that permission be granted to us to make say nine or more holes in the turf – that is the depth of turf only, measuring four inches in diameter in or about the valley leading down from the Fever Hospital.

'It is also essential to roll the turf for a space of say nine feet on each side of the holes. For the granting of such privileges, we are willing to pay such nominal sum of money as may be agreed upon.'

That historic document is dated June 10th, 1891. It was signed by 79 citizens of repute, including merchants, bankers, lawyers, doctors, academics and one cleric.

The Freemen of Newcastle, after due deliberation gave consent to the application upon the signing of a contract to pay them an annual rental of ten guineas.

The petition had then to go before the other mandatory authority, the Corporation's Town Moor Committee. Records show that approval was not immediately given. That led to a second application by the 'City' pioneers on July 14th, 1891 when a deputation led by Dr. Adam Wilson, of Osborne House, Jesmond, presented it in person. On that occasion, the application was successful. Dr. Wilson asked to sink holes in the area of the Moor leading to the Smallpox Hospital, between the Cowhill Road and the footpath leading from the Northern Terrace to the old Grandstand. In order to establish the ownership rights of the land for the new course, the Corporation asked for the sum of one shilling to be paid annually. However, the Town Moor Committee pointed out to Dr. Wilson that its consent would have to be approved by a full meeting of the Newcastle Council.

The matter came before the Newcastle Council on October 19th, 1891 and it soon became clear that there was strong opposition to the plan to construct a golf course. Ald. J. Newton claimed that the building of a course would be just as dangerous as the 'houghing' bowling track, and should be classified as such.

Bowling was a plebian pastime whereas golf was an aristocratic game. . . . If the Council was objecting to the new bowling track, as suggested, they should make it clear they did not accord any privileges to class.

The Mayor informed the Council members that the Freemen had agreed to a golfing experiment on condition 'that the moment the game ceased, the wells for the balls should be stopped up'.

However, some council members could see no harm in the plan. Coun. A. Wilson said that golf was no more dangerous than any other outside sport, and he would object if the Council classed it as dangerous.

Sir B. C. Browne declared that golf was perfectly safe if ordinary care was exercised by the players.

But opponents of building the course were fervent in their objections. Aldermen Stephens and Newton refused to withdraw their objections, claiming they had witnessed golfing accidents on both Whitley and Alnmouth courses when members of the public were the victims.

The row in the council chamber was resolved by a compromise decision. The Council voted themselves the power to prevent bowling and other dangerous games, except on that part of the Moor especially appropriated for the purpose. The plan to build the course was said to fall into the latter category, so the application succeeded.

Later, a second deputation from the 'City G.C.' saw the Town Moor management committee and gave an undertaking that their golfers would cause no danger to members of the public frequenting the Moor, and that 'golf balls will be carried and not played across the roads of the Moor'. The deputation also confirmed arrangements 'to fill up holes on the greens whenever the red flags were not shown'. The old 'City' minute books make no reference to the willingness of members to wear red coats when playing the Moor; but it was common practice on some golf courses in those far-off days.

Having succeeded with all the permissions to construct a course, the 'City G.C.' pioneers now turned their attention to employing professional help in laying out the new course. It says much for the initiative and far-sightedness of the 'City' planners, that they went to the Mecca of golf, St. Andrews to discuss the project with the venerable master himself, Tom Morris Senior. He agreed a contract and in October 1891 travelled to Newcastle and laid out the first course of the City of Newcastle Club.

Old Tom meticulously designed and planned 18 holes on the Town Moor, after which he stood back and told the 'City' pioneers: 'This could become one of the best inland greens (courses) in the country'.

There is no record of the fee paid to him, or the lay-out of course features or bunkers. But an indication of the type of course he liked to design is given in an edition of the magazine, 'GOLF', published at that time in the form of a letter, in which he discussed the criteria for golf course design in general.

One hundred years ago, these were the thoughts of the man who was reputed to know as much about the game of golf as any man in the world. Tom Morris wrote:

'If you have so many miles of ground you can put holes down at say, from 100 to 500 yards, varying them accordingly. The breadth may vary from 50 to 100 yards.' He thought that trees as part of a golf course were not necessary. 'The digging of bunkers and of a whin or two would serve as hazards to all players' he discoursed.

On the question of costing the job, Mr. Morris said that likely costs for laying out greens would be some £5 per green. If a course had to be cleared of gorse bushes or whins, then the likely cost would be some £200 in all. Nice to remember that our first course was designed by 'The Pope of St. Andrews' who had won the Open Championship four times by the time he visited Newcastle and the Moor.

The course he designed on the Moor measured more than 6,000 yards. With all the limitations provided by a newly laid-out course, hickory shafted clubs and gutta-percha balls, it proved a considerable challenge.

Tom Morris' final words before departing from the Town Moor were: 'It could become one of the best inland courses in England, time alone being required to perfect it as the most exacting inland course that a golfer could desire'.

Judging by the early competition returns, the new course turned out to be just as exacting as the old master had predicted.

The 'City' Club now had to search for a man to be appointed as their first Professional. Into the heartland of golf, Scotland, they travelled again and signed up Tom Fernie from Ardeer.

He came with the title of Professional and Course Supervisor at the City of Newcastle Club, with greens staff reporting to him. In addition to his shop and a workshop, he was provided with a house next to the clubhouse in Claremont Road known as Chimney Mills.

This old windmill was a city landmark belonging to W. B. Reid and Son, owners of the Leazes Brewery and a wine and spirits business, who had used the building as a corn mill. In its day, the windmill was a building of great beauty with five large sails and a lovely dome.

It was a stroke of genius to convert this beautiful old mill into a golfing clubhouse. Apart from its close proximity to the Town Moor course, its towering height gave it commanding views over the Moor and the course. The *pièce de résistance* was the creation of a glass observation gallery at the apex of the building, (which disappeared some years ago).

The lower floor of the windmill housed the 'club room' with bar, plus conveniences and the locker room. A handsome staircase led to the first floor which was furnished as a lounge and reading room. Another floor housed a full length snooker table. The mill tower contained eight beautifully fashioned windows, affording good views of the city as well as the Moor.

According to old records, the total cost of the conversion and re-furbishment was some £1,500, a staggeringly high sum for those days. It is understood that W. B. Reid was sympathetic to the idea of starting up a golf club, bearing much of the conversion charge himself.

At any rate, whatever the cost, it appears to have been money well spent as the new clubhouse won admirers at once. Visitors to the 'City G.C.' went away to speak of 'one of the handsomest clubhouses in the kingdom'.

The two 'City' members who were hyperactive in supervising and pushing this conversion through were J. B. Pease, the President and S. F. Bates, the joint Secretary. They were backed up by other officers of the City Golf Club who formed the first committee. Here are their names:

COMMITTEE NO. 1 – 1891

Captain: Dr. Adam Wilson

President: J. W. Pease

Joint Secs: S. F. Bates and J. B. Radcliffe

Treasurer: R. T. Thompson

Messrs. F. W. Wyndham, G. F. Charlton, C. G. Ross, E. L. Orde, Dr. W. T. Wilson, A. H. Marsh, C. W. Muir, Capt. J. Stewart, J. Tennant, Dr. Black, Dr. E. W. Wilson, Dr. G. W. Ridley and J. Brigg.

Although the 'City G.C.' was a brand new club in 1891, it had attracted leading Newcastle citizens from different walks of life as members, who, in the first year totalled just over 100. The first members' roll shows that it embraced, also, numbers of City Councillors and Freemen of Newcastle, thus ensuring a sense of self-protection on the course it rented. Even then it was not always plain-sailing. An early club minute shows that when the Greens Committee wanted to re-locate several holes into an area less frequented by the public they ran into opposition. The Steward's Committee of the Freeman objected 'because the planned area for the new holes is one of the few quiet parts left for the cows to graze in'.

Throughout their tenure on the Town Moor, the presence of cattle on or near the golf course was an insurmountable problem. The Freemen's cows could not legally be moved elsewhere; they grazed on the Moor by virtue of an Act of Parliament – and it would take a fresh Act of Parliament to get rid of them! As a result, it was necessary to introduce protection against the cattle. Most greens were protected by the erection of wire fencing all the way round.

Sometimes, apart from cattle grazing alongside golfers, there were horses to contend with. The Town Moor with its 1,200 acres – the largest open moor within any city boundary in the country – was an invitation to horse-riders to gallop their mounts across the Moor.

Then there was another major nuisance to golfers in those early days of the club – the Cowhill Fair Week. This horse and cattle fair was one of the biggest in the country – as well known as Nottingham's Goose Fair. As well as the animals, large crowds arrived in wagons from all parts of the region. There was no alternative but to suspend 'City' golf for that period. In the wake of the local fair, came the repairs to the turf, all highly frustrating to 'City' golfers.

There were other worries for the 'City G.C.' Committee to face up to. A few years after play commenced on the Moor, the Army Command announced a plan to build a rifle range close to one of the holes on the course. During the same period, the 'City G.C.' Chairman reported to committee that members of the Royal Artillery had been seen drilling on the golf course. A strong letter of complaint to the Commanding Officer of the Newcastle Barracks quashed both ideas.

Although the 'City' Club was founded in October, 1891 the course could not be brought into a state of readiness until February, 1892 for the first competition.

The competition book shows that this date was February 27th.

On this chill February day, with a North wind blowing, a total of 14 members turned out for this inaugural medal competition. The combination of facing the rigours of a new course, including immature greens, and the windy, wintry weather made good scoring very difficult. In fact only one competitor broke a 100. He was W. G. Black, playing off 6 handicap who tied for first place with A. S. Ferguson playing off 20 handicap. The winning score was nett 92! One has to bear in mind that these competitors were playing a long course with old fashioned clubs and balls made out of gutta percha, hardened and painted white.

If the 14 competitors did not cover themselves in glory, they deserve to be mentioned as taking part in this historic event. The names of the members who played that day:

FIRST 'CITY' COMPETITION – FEBRUARY 27th, 1892

W. G. Black (joint winner)
A. S. Ferguson (joint winner)
A. C. Margary
G. Sutherland
P. Cochrane
E. L. Bates
I. Limont
A. Hunter
A. J. Harrison
I. R. Bolton
A. Wilson
A. H. Marsh
A. Richardson
W. G. Richardson

Chapter II
'THE TESTING YEARS' 1891–1907

Although the City of Newcastle Golf Club was founded in October, 1891 and competitions began four months later, the official opening of the club did not take place until September, 1892.

The new course needed time to settle down, and the 'City' Commitee needed time to plan an opening in the grand manner. The chosen day was September 21st – the day's programme included a banquet in the refurbished club-house and an Open Golf Tournament.

Places of honour at the dining table were accorded to the Mayor of the City, Coun. W. Sutton, the chairmen of the Town Moor Management Committee and the Stewards' Committee of the Freemen. Also present were City Councillors and Freemen and Captains of local golf clubs.

In his inaugural Presidential speech, Mr. J. W. Pease said that on this momentous day for golf in the City of Newcastle it was worth reflecting on the origins of the game. Golf was possibly introduced to Britain from Holland about the year 1400, he said. By 1450 it was well-established in Scotland, thus taking some four centuries to find its way across the borders to Northumberland.

The Mayor of Newcastle – himself a Scot – stated that Newcastle Corporation 'was well disposed to provide for the great population of Newcastle upon Tyne healthy recreation and amusement'. Hence his City Council had extended co-operation in the formation of this new City Golf Club. Responding on behalf of visiting golfers, Mr. J. Lowthian Bell, Captain of Newbiggin G.C. wished good fortune upon the new club and toasted its health.

After the luncheon, members and guests assembled in front of the windmill club-house to be photographed by Mr. James Bacon, professional photographer of Newcastle. The assembly then proceeded to 'the teeing ground' for the inaugural drive-in by the Club President. By all accounts, Mr. Pease got a good one away, long and straight, which purported to be a good omen for the fledgling club.

Then the competition, which had attracted a considerable entry for those days of more than 60 golfers, began. Every golfer was on his mettle trying to win the coveted award of the first President's Gold Medal (played off scratch). But there were also handicap prizes to be won, including seven guineas for the winner in the below 18 handicap section, and a similar sum to be won in the 18–36 handicap section.

The 'City G.C.' had ruled that the winner of the Gold Medal be declared Club Champion and Captain-Elect. As it turned out, the result was a glorious win for the Pease Family. President J. W. Pease was present to applaud the win of his son, J. Beaumont Pease who was elected Captain of the City of Newcastle G.C. in 1892.

Other winners on this special day for the 'City G.C.' included Mr. P. Ismay of Tyneside G.C. (nett 80 playing off 13 handicap); and Mr. M. Whiteford of Newbiggin G.C. (nett 70 playing off 19).

For the first few years, the City golfers were experiencing all the rigours and frustrations of a newly-designed course, immature fairways and tricky greens. Despite all that, members of the 'City' made rapid improvement as the record of matches against other clubs in the area showed.

Only five years after opening the 'City G.C.' was able to field one of the strongest representative teams in the district.

In 1896 the 'City' dished out a hiding to the well-established Berwick (Goswick) Golf Club. Admittedly the match was at home, but the 'City G.C.' won every match and by large margins.

Even allowing for the different team scoring system of those days (each side added up the number of holes won outright by every member of their team, producing an aggregate total) the winning margin of 85 holes sounds hard to believe!

During those early years there were a number of outstanding feats on the 'City' Course, including several holes in one. One rather unusual feat was performed by the 'City' player, W. R. Rumbold, playing off 3 handicap in a 36 hole competition. In the first and second rounds, he twice drove the 234 yard par 4 hole and each time holed the putt, thus recording consecutive eagles at the same hole on the same day.

In those formative years on the Town Moor course, a small number of lady golfers appeared on the scene. Traditionally, it has been thought that women's golf at the 'City' began with the formation of 'The Three Mile Bridge Ladies' Golf Club' on February 2nd, 1925. But it can be said unequivically that women were playing on the old course long before that, as recorded in the club records.

One entry in the 'City Golf Club' balance sheet of 1894 reads: 'Ladies' Club – subscriptions £18 5s. less rent of Fernie's Room, £3 14s.' 'Fernie' is Tom Fernie, first professional at the 'City', who came to Newcastle from Scotland.

Again, in the balance sheet for 1895 there is an entry registering the sum of £20 received from the Ladies Club for subscriptions.

And again, in the 'City G.C.' minute book of May 17th. 1897 is a record of a request from the Ladies Committee of the 'City' Club asking if they can acquire accommodation beginning in 1898. The Club Committee agreed they could, and offered a small committee room facing the Town Moor at an annual charge of 7/6d. The Ladies have a long and glorious history at the City of Newcastle as is shown in a later chapter devoted to them.

THE 'BOBBY JONES' OF THE TOWN MOOR

There was no indication when a good-looking teenage boy with a passion for golf appeared on the Town Moor scene before the turn of the century, that he would turn out to be one of the great golfers of the age.

The then City of Newcastle professional, J. S. Caird, spotted his potential early and took him under his wing. The teenager was James Douglas Edgar who turned out to be a genius for the theory and practice of the game, and after turning professional beat some of the world's best players.

As a young player on the Town Moor he won competitions with the United Workmen's Club who also played on the 'City G.C.' course, later surrendering his amateur status to become Assistant Professional to J. S. Caird. Edgar moved to Gosforth Park as their Professional after learning the craft of club-repairing and club-making.

His first success in the professional ranks was to become French Open Champion in 1914, and he followed that up with other major wins after accepting a post with Druid Hills Golf Club, Atlanta, U.S.A. in 1918.

The brilliant golfing career of Douglas Edgar came to an abrupt and violent end on August 9th, 1921 in Atlanta, when he died as a result of suspected foul play. The full story of this golfing genius from Newcastle upon Tyne is told in a later chapter.

'HALCYON DAYS ON THE MOOR'

'But What of the Club Professional?'

Many club golfers, preoccupied with the daily frustrations of modern life and work are inclined to think of the Club Professional as 'something that goes with the club'. If that is so today, then it was no different in the early days of the 'City G.C.' on the Town Moor. It is a sobering experience to read through the contract between the club and its Professional in 1898.

Mr. J. S. Caird had been appointed as Professional, Club-maker and Caddie Master at a salary of £10 per annum. He was given a free workshop, coals and gas. His duties included:

Manufacturing and repairing clubs.

The handing out and taking-in of members' clubs.

Supervising Caddies and payment of fees.

Cleaning of members' boots.

Running the shop and giving lessons.

'And any other duties required of him for the general welfare of the club'.

While Mr. Caird was 'a servant of the club' he was not paid as such. He was paid the princely retainer of £10 per year – so he turned to the industry of manufacturing and selling clubs to augment his salary. If the club was a biggish one, and the City has always been that, then the Pro. would need to keep an assistant. Mr. Caird would pay his assistants, including J. D. Edgar, out of his own pocket.

Other duties included being present to give lessons to any member so desiring them; to keep stocks of balls and other equipment, and to listen to interminable hard-luck stories and offer, without a fee, thoughts on a quick cure for a fault!

In addition, the Pro. was expected to keep his premises open from early morning to cater for the first couple driving off until late in the evening. Perhaps the contract for the modern Pro. is not as arduous though several of the principles of employment are retained by most clubs, including payment by retainer.

In those far-off days, nearly all members played with caddies. The going rate at the 'City G.C.' at the turn of the century for engaging an experienced caddie was one shilling per round. Out of that sum, the 'City' Professional was allowed to deduct one penny booking fee.

It is somewhat surprising that the paid employee engaged to run the Chimney Mills Clubhouse was a woman. Mrs. J. Shearer's contract combined her duties as Stewardess with that of Caretaker – for which she was paid the sum of ten shillings per week. Though she was allowed to retain all profits on refreshments prepared by her and half the profits on mineral waters sold.

Nevertheless, her duties were demanding to say the least and included the following:

Running the club bar.

Supplying refreshments and food.

Maintaining the club-house in 'thoroughly clean condition'.

Drying all members' clothing as necessary.

'And doing all that is required by the Committee'.

The membership at that time was recorded as 300.

Perhaps it was not surprising if the Stewardess found it hard to cope with such a demanding schedule, coupled with the long hours entailed in such a job. One entry in the 'City G.C.' Minute Book states that when the Newcastle Inspector of Nuisances carried out an inspection of the clubhouse he found 'That the smells in the lavatories were caused by want of water'. One has to remember the limitations of the public water supply in those days.

The old minute books of the Club reflect aspects of the regime operating before the turn of the century. One entry for 1897 shows the sum of £2-1s-8d paid to the local authority as a contribution towards the Poor Rates. (That was a compulsory payment levied on the Club to help maintain the poor of the parish). Another entry tells of the 'City G.C.' having to seek the permission of the Freemen to build two bunkers (Permission was granted on payment of a nominal sum). Another minute reveals how the 'City G.C.' greenkeeper was sharply rebuked by the committee for asking the United Workmen's Club for an honourarium (United golfers played on the 'City' course). Mr. J. Peggie, the greenkeeper was told by the 'City G.C.' that his services were rendered to the 'City G.C.' only, and he was out of order.

A SCHISM AT THE 'CITY G.C.'

The year 1898 was a trying one for the 'City' of Newcastle G.C. Despite the successful launch of the club and the popularity of golf, all was not well. The problem centred on the course lying on an open moor, on which public encroachment could not be stopped. Seven years after the start of the club, public interference with members' golf caused a crisis.

A nucleus of 'City' members were also disenchanted by the restrictive regulations imposed on the golf course as a result of it being an area of public land, supervised by two landlords (The Newcastle Corporation and the Freemen of the City). It was difficult if not impossible to plant new trees, grow rough at fairway sides and make a sufficient number of bunkers. There were some features on the course – the 'Dynamite Hole', the Fever Hospital and the Craghall Byrne. But apart from the odd bunker, playing members could be fairly wild through the fairways without incurring penalty shots.

So in 1897 an unofficial committee of interested members was set up to consider and inquire into various possible sites for a new golf course. The members, some 130 in all, finally settled their sights on Gosforth Park where, some seven years before, Newcastle Races had been transferred from the Town Moor.

'The Park' offered two main advantages: the area possessed fine features, woodlands, copses and other interesting hazards such as the railings surrounding the race-track! The second advantage was the location of the Park with its advantages when it came to transport, and its proximity to Killingworth Station.

So by 1898 this considerable exodus of golfers from the 'City' had taken place, causing all kinds of problems for the golfers left behind to carry the 'City' colours on the Town Moor.

The biggest worry now for the 'City' Committee was lack of finance. The loss of subscriptions from 130 members was a wounding blow.

The rental to be paid for the clubhouse alone amounted to £170.00 which was more than half the total monies received from subscriptions in 1898.

In order to stay solvent, the club requested the rent paid to W. B. Reid, the brewer, to be reduced. The 'City' Committee was shocked to learn that the landlord refused to grant their request. He pointed out to the club that his company had made a large outlay in helping to convert the mill into a golf clubhouse. In desperation, the 'City G.C.' Committee sent a deputation to see Mr. Reid and to explain the critical financial situation of the Club which was threatened with closure. It was then that the landlord relented and knocked a fair sum off the annual rental.

That ensured the survival of the 'City' as a golf club, though the disturbance caused by this breakaway movement was an unhappy interlude in the early history of the club. However, the 'City G.C.' gradually repaired the damage and built up its membership again; it was largely due to the sterling efforts of the committee and officers like J. B. Ratcliffe, the Captain, and J. W. Pease, the Club President.

'CITY G.C.' PIONEERS CALLED PEASE
John William Pease – First President
J. Beaumont Pease – First Club Champion

The family of Pease played an important role in the early days of the 'City' of Newcastle G.C., from the beginnings on the Town Moor and for years after that extending to the new headquarters at the Three Mile Bridge.

John William Pease, the first President of the Club in 1891 was part of a well-known Newcastle banking company called Hodgkin, Barnet, Spence and Pease with head office located in Collingwood Street. As President of the 'City G.C.' he played the first shot from the first tee to open officially the Town Moor course. He also gave the club's oldest trophy, the Pease Gold Medal, in 1892.

After his death in 1901, the local banking company was sold to Lloyds Bank though J. Beaumont Pease (son of J. W. Pease) continued to work for the new owners. In 1906, Beaumont Pease arranged for the purchase of Lambton's Bank in Newcastle which is now the Lloyds Bank of Grey Street. Then in 1923, Beaumont Pease was appointed Chairman of Lloyds Bank – a post he held for the next 22 years . . .

J. Beaumont ('Monty') Pease was equally as successful on the golf course, becoming an outstanding player. He also played his part in administration, following in his father's footsteps as Club President, a post he held for many years. When the 'City G.C.' moved from the Moor to the Three Mile Bridge in 1907, Beaumont Pease was one of the guiding hands over-seeing the transfer.

But it was as a player that Beaumont Pease really came into his own.

He was the first winner of the Club Championship at the 'City G.C.' and the first winner of the Northumberland County Championship in its inaugural year of 1907.

In his golfing career, Beaumont Pease played out of both the 'City' and Alnmouth before moving South. The Pease family, many years ago owned a house called 'Nether Grange', the front door and stables of which opened directly onto to the Alnmouth course. His family provided the land for the club-house which was built at a cost of some £500.

But whether it was the 'City' or Alnmouth, Beaumont Pease was always the golfer the others had to beat. He became an English International, and for many years was a strong competitor in the Amateur Championship, competing until the age of 72! In fact Beaumont Pease continued his sound golf game until the day he died in 1950 aged 81.

In his later years, playing at Todmorton, near Banbury he went round that course in his age until the day he died. When he was 71, he returned a card of 69 for 18 holes. This was a golfer who earlier in his life had played off a plus handicap for years.

Beaumont Pease was also a hole in 1 specialist. The present Lord Wardington of Banbury, Oxon, his son, writes:

'I think he did 11 holes in 1 during his life – Alnmouth taught him to be incredibly accurate, And he is the only man I've ever heard of who did a hole in 1 when he had to! This was at Pau in the Pyrenees where the last hole is a short one and where he was giving a stroke. His opponent played first and laid it stone dead.' His father's shot was the ace!

In 1931 Beaumont Pease was invited to become Captain of the Royal and Ancient Club of St. Andrews. In 1936 he was elevated to the Peerage for his service to banking. It was then that he took the title of Baron Wardington with the family seat located at Wardington, near Banbury. He also served for several years as P.G.A. President from 1947, and officiated at the Ryder Cup Match played at Ganton, near Scarborough in 1949.

The present Lord Wardington writes that he was playing with father on the day he died. '. . . We got to the 10th hole where he said he did'nt feel so good; so we went home and he died in his sleep'.

The 'City' Club possesses a prized link with the Peases: the hickory-shafted driver used by J. B. Pease on the Town moor course and crafted by Tom Fernie, the first 'City G.C.' professional.

EARLY GOLF BALLS
Rulings at the 'City' of Newcastle G.C.

When golf began in earnest at the 'City G.C.' in the late 1890's, the popular ball among members and widely accepted nation-wide was the gutta-percha, familiarly known as 'the gutty'. Ball manufacturers obtained this substance from the Malaysian gutta-percha tree.

It was a reddish brown, horn-like substance which could be softened by heat and moulded into the shape of a golf ball, and which set rock-hard when cooled.

By the close of the 19th-century, this ball had taken on the modern look, fashioned with indentations. Its hard surface enabled the golfer to strike the ball further, though compared to today's ball it possessed certain limitations.

The only other ball then played by a minority of 'City G.C.' golfers was the 'Eclipse'. It consisted of a mixture of rubber, cork and metal fillings, and did not have much success.

The introduction of the first 'modern' golf ball – the 'Haskell' manufactured in America – caused the 'City' Greens Committee to give a ruling on it in 1902. The 'Haskell' ball was a real break through: it was composed of strips of elastic wound tightly round a liquid filled rubber core inside a casing of gutta-percha. It was easier to strike from the ground and travelled much further than any previous ball, though in 1902 the supply was limited.

The 'City' golfers who had managed to obtain this new ball held a distinct advantage over other competitors who had not, causing a ruling to appear on the 'City G.C.' notice board barring the use of the 'Haskell' until further notice.

By 1903 the supply of this imported ball had improved, and the 'City' ban was lifted.

During the 1930's, further improvements were carried out in the production of the golf ball; and 'City' players became familiar with brand names like 'Silver King' and 'Bromford'. Later a ball appeared that was to sweep most other competitors aside – the Dunlop '65'. In its original size of 1.62 diameter, later known as the smaller ball, it was the favourite ball of 'City G.C.' players for many years. The same company also produced a cheaper version, known as the 'Warwick' which was also popular.

When, during the 1970's there was talk in high places of making the larger American ball of 1.68 diameter compulsory, there were mutterings of disagreement at the 'City' Club. Many players favoured the smaller ball; it travelled just as far and was not so susceptible to high winds. As all golfers know, the larger ball won the day and is now universally accepted.

THE DECISION TO QUIT THE MOOR

Following the breakaway of some 130 City golfers from the Moor in 1898 to form The Northumberland Golf Club, it was hoped to improve the members' lot on the Town Moor course by developing the lay-out and curtailing the encroachment of non-members playing golf on the 'City' course. The Committee did their best, but in the end they found that trying to run a private golf club on public land was a contradiction in terms.

So it was hardly surprising that in April, 1906 the City of Newcastle Golf Club took the wise decision of looking for pastures new. The Club minutes record that many locations were visited and inspected, including High Gosforth Farm (terms unsatisfactory); a large farmland at Ponteland; a plot of ground at Kenton Station; and the Grange Farm site at Gosforth. The Club Committee were in favour of taking out a lease, which was offered by the owners of the Grange Farm – land professionally deemed suitable for the construction of a golf course, with access to the Great North Road at Three Mile Bridge. So early in the 1900's the 'City's' association with the Town Moor began drawing to a close. At the beginning of golf on this magnificent open space, there had been great optimism about the future. The opening of the course had prompted one local journalist to write: 'It brings with it, in its advance the blessing of mental and physical enjoyment which the mysterious cult so liberally confers on its students'.

No doubt there were many golden memories of the early play on the Moor – but by 1906 public encroachment and congestion on the course, had removed much of the members' enjoyment.

The special meeting of the City of Newcastle Golf Club to confirm their departure from the Town Moor took place at the County Hotel, Newcastle on March 19th, 1907. Dr. Adam Wilson, the club chairman told a large body of members that in the short history of the club they had arrived at a crisis. When they commenced golfing on the Town Moor some 16 years earlier only ' a small body of men' found pleasure in taking up the game. Since then, the game had grown in popularity so that at the start of 1907 the 'City' boasted 338 playing members.

The good Dr. declared: 'Not only that, but a vast horde of undisciplined people who owe allegiance to no club took up the pursuit of the game on the Moor'. He added that some of those incomers knew neither the principles nor the etiquette of the game. He was optimistic about the choice of the Three Mile Bridge; a lease had been tentatively agreed with the Bainbridge family for a yearly rental of some £400.00. The pastures new would enable members to play golf on good turf amid 'pleasurable surrounds'. Golf was a game he would recommend to anyone. 'The more golfing members got, the less physic they would require!' was the Doctor's diagnosis for good health.

Chapter III

ARRIVAL AT THE THREE MILE BRIDGE

Golf at the New Venue

The City of Newcastle Golf Club transferred itself, lock, stock and barrel from the Town Moor to the Three Mile location in August, 1907, after signing a lease with the widow of John T. Bainbridge. The annual rental was £400, due in two instalments.

Before the club moved in, they had engaged the services of one of the great golfers of the age – Harry Vardon – to advise on the design of the course.

The signature on the first tenancy agreement was that of John Henry Boyd, Hon. Solicitor to the Club who was a founder member. His son, another John Boyd, later followed in his father's footsteps at the 'City' as Hon. Solicitor and still attends the 'City' today.

It was fitting that at the opening of the new course on August 10th, 1907 J. Beaumont Pease, Club President struck the first drive down the fairway, carrying on the tradition of the Pease family from the Town Moor. Playing alongside the President in the four ball was the Club Secretary, Mr. James Potts who was unaware of the drama that was about to unfold. His drive off the first tee struck a death blow. His well-struck shot hit a crow in flight and it fell to the ground. The secretary attended to it and took it back to the clubhouse in the hope that it might survive. In fact it died. The unlucky bird, standing in the way of history, was stuffed, placed in a glass case with the 'missile' that felled it, and given a place of honour in the clubhouse.

In those far-off days, the 'City' course was set amid picturesque, rural surroundings. The urbanisation of Newcastle upon Tyne had not yet extended to the Three Mile Bridge; the horse-drawn trams did not operate as far as the clubhouse entrance.

The unspoiled countryside was alive with game of all kinds. Some might say that the 'City' then was 'a golfing paradise' – there were no irritating traffic noises from nearby main roads; no transistor radios or chimes from ice-cream vans; no roar of multi-jet aircraft passing overheard. If a 'City' golfer was distracted in those olden days it was more likely than not caused by a rabbit or hare scuttling across his path.

The owner of these green acres, Mrs. Bainbridge lived with her two daughters in grand style in the Grange Farm, the property still standing in its own grounds behind the present second green.

The contract lease taken out with Mrs. Bainbridge has some interesting clauses. They included the following:

> Sunday golf not permitted.
> The owner retains the right to tether a milking cow.
> The right for sheep to graze on certain areas.

The right to fish in the byrne and shoot game.

The protection and preservation of birds' nests.

The golfers who played in these idyllic surroundings were dressed in Tweed jackets and plus fours or breeches; their clubs were hickory-shafted; and their golf bags were much smaller as many golfers at the turn of the century played with an average of seven or eight clubs.

There is no doubt that the Committee of the 1900's made an excellent choice in the Three Mile Bridge site. It was situated on the old Great North Road and public transport to the course would not be long in stepping up services; the soil and grass were good agricultural land which lent itself to conversion to a good golf course; and the location was suitable for building a clubhouse by the main road, as well as homes for the head greenkeeper and clubhouse staff. For in those days the 'City' staff lived on the premises.

A contract was struck with a Newcastle building company to build the clubhouse. Later, the building firm of Stephen Easten built the sun lounge extension in 10 weeks for some £475.

In addition, stables were built to accommodate horses as well as an equipment shed. Before the application of the internal combustion engine, much of the heavy work on the course was performed by horses who pulled the gangs and cutters. All the greens were finely hand-cut.

The 'City' Professional, J. S. Caird played an important part, along with Harry Vardon in supervising the preparation of the new course. Apart from other duties, Mr. Caird continued to organise the caddies, who still received 11d. per round (one penny going to the Professional as a booking fee). He also collected green fees which, in 1907 were as follows:

VISITORS: GREEN FEES
Per day – 2/- (weekdays)
Per day, Saturdays and Sundays and Bank Holidays 10/-
Weekly ticket, visitors living outside 20 mile radius 7/6d. (Weekends and Bank Holidays, – play with Members only.)
Visitors not allowed to start before 11 a.m. on competition days.

One revealing minute from the Club's records states that women were employed in 1907 to weed the 18th and other greens. This attitude to women's employment is not to be taken as that of the 'City' Committee towards lady golfers, though it has to be stated that women were kept at a distance after the Club moved to the Three Mile Bridge. For example, the Club could not allow them to form their own Ladies' Club or section for many years.

The Committee minute of July 30th, 1907 reads: 'Ladies: wives, sisters and daughters of members and ladies playing with them, or with members are entitled to the privileges of the course free. All other ladies must pay green fees and be introduced by a member. All lady players to sign the visitors' book and obtain tickets'.

The Committee also issued further regulations affecting the ladies: they could not use all clubhouse rooms, only the rooms 'set apart for their use'; a match in which a lady was playing was to allow a match in which no lady was playing to pass; ladies were not to play on Sundays, and those playing on Saturdays could not start before 11 a.m.

More than 80 years ago the par for the course was known as the Bogey score. At the 'City' course the bogey was 82, that is 42 out and 40 back. In the first nine holes, there were two par 6's and four par 5's, and on the back nine, one par 6 and four par 5's. With the course measuring some 6,062 yards with several challenging features, including the burn coming into play at several holes, it presented a tough proposition. Especially if one takes into account the quality of the equipment used in those days. Swing-weighted match sets of 14 clubs; steel shafts; non-slip grips; the wedge; long-distance golf balls; and other golfing aids were things of the future.

There is no record in the Club minutes of what Harry Vardon thought of playing for the first time on the course designed by him. It must have given him considerable pleasure, as he returned to play at the 'City' on several subsequent occasions. This close association with Vardon is a signal honour for the 'City', as he was reputed to be one of the finest – if not the finest – golfers of his era. His record included those six Open Championship victories; and, of course, the Vardon grip became the most popular grip for golfers the world over. For seven years he was Pro. at Ganton which was also founded in 1891.

The 'City' records show that in May, 1908 Harry Vardon was back at the 'City' again to play an exhibition match against another all-time great, James Braid. The winner of this 36 hole match is not recorded, but this professional clash attracted a large crowd at the Three Mile Bridge who paid one shilling each for the privilege of watching the masters play.

When the Club was officially opened at its new headquarters in 1907, the Committee had tried to bring three Open Champions together. They made an approach to Arnaud Massey, the fine French golfer who made headlines by becoming the first overseas player to win the 'Open' in 1907. Perhaps he could not be bothered to travel to Tyneside after his great win at Hoylake; or perhaps the appearance fee of £25 was not thought to be sufficient. His reply to the 'City' was negative.

The idea was dropped, although two other 'Open' champions – James Braid and Harry Vardon – had intimated they could probably take part in an inaugural match.

In those days, the rules of golf included playing 'The Stymie'; this was a very tricky shot indeed as it took place on the green. The rule said in effect, that if an opponent's ball lay between the hole and the line of the ball in play on the green, then the shot or putt was to be played as the balls lay. Jumping over a stationary ball on the green sounds a frightening business; there was no other option if the player wanted to save a shot. This rule applied for many years, and John Boyd can remember reading clubhouse notices in the 1920's reminding players to take care on the green in playing the shot, and not to cut the green up. When that rule was rescinded it must have had universal approval.

In the first decade on the Grange course of the 'City', several famous names came to look at and play the 'City'. In 1910 another 'Open' winner, George Duncan, came to play a challenge match against James Braid, who had won several Open Championships already.

Club minutes reveal that each player was paid an appearance fee of ten guineas plus travelling expenses.

Like any new laid-out course, a span of time is necessary in order to allow the course to settle down and for greens to mature. According to the local newspapers of the day, the course was barely ready for serious play when the first competition was held on August 10th. 1907. A report from the 'Newcastle Daily Journal', August 12th, 1907: 'Members of the City of Newcastle Golf Club took possession of their new headquarters and inaugurated play over the new course on Saturday. Matches were played but the greens as yet being immature and the going heavy in places, no good returns were registered. The formal opening of the club was deferred.'

The results of that first competition show that the winner was A. V. Newton who returned a nett 85 playing of 18 handicap. His 'sweep money' was 16s. 8d. The lowest gross of the day was 86 by J. C. Seymour, a scratch player.

Another contemporary newspaper report, discovered in 'The Sporting Man' claimed that the new 'City' course had been opened too early. 'The course, though, will certainly become one of the finest in the county and should prove an excellent school for 'City' golfers who have little experience of straight driving. (An allusion to the wide open spaces of the old course on the Town Moor).

The same sporting journalist, reviewing the story of the 'City' Club since its inception in 1891 was, nevertheless impressed by the overall standard of play by 'City' golfers. 'The existence of the 'City G.C.' has resulted in a real stronghold of golf in Newcastle with players quite capable of holding their own in the best of company' he commented.

THE 'CITY' AND 'NEWCASTLE UNITED'

For many years, the City of Newcastle Golf Club had close links with the United Workmens' Golf Club, both playing on the Town Moor course.

The year after the 'City' was founded, and after establishing a headquarters and clubhouse at Chimney Mills, the inaugural meeting of the United Workmen's Golf Club took place. The meeting was held in Lockharts Cocoa Rooms in Clayton Street, Newcastle, and the 'City' Professional, Thomas Fernie, took the chair. After this artisan group of golfers had established itself, and with the help of Mr. Fernie, arrangements were made for United to commence play on the 'City G.C.' course.

The Workmen's Club was founded on June 4th 1892, and their first competition was staged a week later under their first Captain, Mr. J. F. Thomson. At this period of golfing history it was fairly common to find artisan groups of golfers playing as a club within a club. The arrangement seemed to work quite satisfactorily, and 'City G.C.' minutes record inter-club matches taking place from time to time.

An example of the co-operation existing between the clubs is a 'City' minute of May 3rd, 1905 which reads: 'The Secretary was approached by the Workmen's Club who asked to sandwich in at the first tee on the following Saturday'. The 'City' Committee agreed to give courtesy between 1 p.m. to 3 p.m. on that day.

As golf became more popular in Newcastle and district, both clubs suffered from the encroachment of non-members onto the course, many of whom escaped without paying green fees.

Also with increasing membership of the 'City' Club, and the coming of the five-and-a-half day week Saturday afternoons became prime-time for playing. From 1903, the 'City' Committee appointed a Starter to supervise the playing order on the first tee on Saturday afternoons. For that duty, he was paid the princely sum of two shillings.

When the 'City' Golf Club decided in 1906 that they could tolerate the intrusion of non-members onto the Moor no longer, the United Club agreed to take over the running and maintenance of the course from the following year when the 'City' moved out.

United, having some time before changed their name to the 'Newcastle United Golf Club' also took over the clubhouse in the old windmill in Claremont Road. The club remained there until 1975 when they transferred to new headquarters at Cowgate.

If golf in the 1900's was a game for the rich and well-to-do of the district, it meant an exclusive club like the 'City' did not have a large membership. As a result, there were fewer members to meet the continuing cash calls necessary to sustain a spacious and new headquarters at the Three Mile Bridge.

After just four years at the new headquarters, the 'City' was faced with financial difficulties. It was agreed to raise the annual subscription from one guinea to three guineas, and entrance fee for new members to a new level of ten guineas. The bank overdraft stood at the sizeable sum of £2,000.

By 1912 the Club Committee decided it was time for drastic action, and in that year abandoned the policy of exclusiveness. In August the Club accepted 140 new playing members in one go, an action unthought of only four years before. A few weeks later, another group of applications was discussed by the Club committee. On this occasion nearly 40 more golfers were admitted to the Club, bringing the total membership up to 502!

Of all the expenses born in running the City of Newcastle Club, including paying rates and insurance, greens staff, professional and clubhouse staff, the biggest by far was the annual rental for the lease of the land. The yearly burden of over £400 for rental alone for the course was expected to be increased at any time. In those days that was a considerable sum.

By increasing the membership and with tight and shrewd management at this difficult period, the bank overdraft was reduced by about £1,000 at the beginning of World War I.

The rigours of a country at war were to have serious repercussions on the running of the Club. . . . . the story of this second financial crisis is told in a later chapter.

City Of Newcas

Three Mile Bridg

COMPETITION .... DATE..

PLAYERS: ....

Marker	Hole	Yards	Bogey	Gross	Nett
	1	360	5		
	2	225	4		
	3	370	5		
	4	445	5		
	5	180	3		
	6	520	6		
	7	160	3		
	8	420	5		
	9	470	6		
	OUT	3150	42		

Length of Course: 6062 yds. Bogey for Course: 8

Markers Signature: ....

Players Signature: ....

A facsimile of the first score-card at the Three Mile Bridge course in 1907, setting the bogey (par) at 82 (42 out and 40 back). Note the number of 'par' 5's and 'par' 6's. The 'par' 3 of only 97 yards on the old 15th must be one of the shortest played short holes in the country.

E GOLF CLUB

Year – 1907

..H/CAP...... STROKES RECEIVED

Marker	Hole	Yards	Bogey	Gross	Nett
	10	290	4		
	11	200	3		
	12	430	5		
	13	440	5		
	14	380	5		
	15	97	3		
	16	400	5		
	17	500	6		
	18	175	4		
	IN	2912	40		
	OUT	3150	42		
	TOTAL	6062	82		
		HANDICAP			
		NETT			

James Douglas Edgar, Assistant to 'The City' Professional on the Town Moor, J. S. Caird. Edgar was recognised as one of the master golfers of his day. He had victories over Braid, Ray, Taylor and Duncan and once beat the immortal Harry Vardon by six shots to win the French 'Open'. Edgar won the Royal Canadian 'Open' twice, defeating the great Bobby Jones. He also came within a shot of winning the American PGA Championship (three-putting the last green to give Jock Hutchinson the title).
(Photo reproduced by kind permission of Michael Newrick of Gosforth.)

Chapter IV

THE DOUGLAS EDGAR SAGA

Master Golfer from Newcastle upon Tyne

The story of James Douglas Edgar, encompassing historic chapters in this game of golf, is worth telling in some detail as he had connections with both the City of Newcastle and Newcastle United Clubs in the Town Moor days, and later the Northumberland Club at Gosforth Park.

He died and was buried in the United States of America. On his gravestone on Lot 679, Section 14 of the Westview Cemetery of Atlanta, Georgia is the epitaph:

J. DOUGLAS EDGAR
September 30th, 1885 – August 9th, 1921
A Native of England

'ONE OF THE GREAT GOLFERS OF THE AGE'

That is an outstanding tribute to any golfer, though reading through his achievements in the world of golf it is nothing more than justified. When Douglas Edgar, born and bred in Newcastle, first came to play golf on the Town Moor he was very young indeed. But by the age of 17 he was winning competitions with the United Workmen's Club, and catching the eye of the 'City' Professional, J. S. Caird. Caird was said to be nothing more than a competent professional golfer, but he was a good club-maker and excellent teacher. He decided that he would teach young Edgar everything he knew.

The young player responded so well and was so enthusiastic, that Caird invited him to become Assistant Professional to the 'City' Club, which he accepted.

When a group of 'City' players had broken away from the Moor and helped to form the new Club at The Park in 1898, Caird was asked to become their professional, an offer he declined. However, he did agree to help them develop their new course.

A few years later, when the Northumberland Club was again looking for a professional, Caird suggested his assistant on the Moor, Douglas Edgar. Terms were agreed and Edgar crossed the road and took his first job as a Club Professional.

He was only in his 20th year, he settled in well, was pleasant and well-liked but inclined to be a drinker, and some said that he was a favourite among the ladies.

By this time Edgar was the complete Professional – a good club-maker and club repairer, a sound player with an easy swing with plenty of power in his drives, and an excellent teacher. Despite all that, by May of 1911 the 'Park' Committee had had enough of him and asked him 'to look for another berth'. It was said that Edgar's weakness was his temperament, though on the golf course in competition it was always under control. In the end, he did not leave the club. A Northumberland G.C. minute of February, 1912 reported that as Edgar had not found a suitable position, his notice would be withdrawn 'as he has shown improvement in his attention to his duties'.

During these years at the 'Park', Edgar had played with some success in Professional tournaments without ever winning. That situation was rectified with a vengeance in 1914 when he beat some of the world's best to win the French Open Championship. The great Harry Vardon tailed him by six shots; other famous names beaten that day included Braid, Taylor, Ray and Duncan.

At the outbreak of the Great War, Edgar joined the Royal Army Medical Corps and was fortunate to be given a local posting. This allowed him, in his time off, to turn up at the Northumberland Club and give lessons to anyone who was around.

Some years later, as the war drew to a close and Edgar was back at the 'Park' as their Professional, he ran foul of the Northumberland G.C. Committee, and drink was said to be the cause. The story goes that Edgar was invited into the Clubhouse by some members, and his behaviour caused offence. As a result of that row, he gave his notice in and decided to emigrate to the United States of America.

There he secured a professional appointment at the Druids Hill Golf Club in Atlanta. He could hardly have known the cruel stroke of fate that lay waiting for him. That was sometime in the future.

Meanwhile, the new Club of Druids Hill proved amenable and Edgar – a handsome and moody man – became popular with both men and women members.

On the field of play, J. Douglas Edgar was about to begin a successful tournament run against some of the world's finest golfers. In 1919, he entered and won in great style the Royal Canadian Championship, competing against top Americans. He then entered and nearly won the American PGA Championship, being a close runner-up. Next he entered and won the U.S. Southern Open Championship. In 1920 he won the Royal Canadian Open for the second year running.

Douglas Edgar's successful technique in major competition caused the sports writers to sing his praises. One sports journalist wrote of him: 'He is an artist in golf in the same way that Caruso is in music. When the mood is upon him, he can tear apart any golf course'.

This was the Douglas Edgar who, early in his career nearly gave up his golf to become a farmer. He decided against it when one day he discovered the secret of the game of golf which he called 'The Movement of Hitting through the Gate'. Edgar's movement in fact was the consolidation of the modern golf swing. In 1920 he published his definitive instructional book called 'The Gate to Golf'. Apart from knowledge imparted from the book, the purchaser also received a pack containing the 'gate' which could be taken to the course for practice. The 'gate' consisted of two shaped pieces of wood, pegged to the ground which formed the perfect path for the club-head to travel through to produce the classic 'In to Out Swing'. Many American golfers benefited, including Professionals.

Edgar's book, published more than 70 years ago was acclaimed as a major work on the teaching of the game of golf. Tommy Armour, one of the masters of the game said that 'The Gate to Golf' was the best book there was (even though Armour had written a master-piece on golf instruction himself).

The Douglas Edgar saga is also fascinating because of his links with the immortal Bobby Jones. Jones was only a young man while Edgar was a seasoned Professional when they often played together in Atlanta, Georgia where Bobby was born in 1902. He started his golf on the East Lake Course in Atlanta whereas Douglas Edgar was Professional at Druids Hill Golf Club.

One is tempted to think that the young Bobby Jones might have learned a thing or two from the master craftsman called Edgar; after all, they not only played together in Atlanta but also travelled together to various national tournaments.

In 1919, when Edgar won the Royal Canadian Open, he was 34 and Jones was still under 20. In that Open Championship, which featured a crack field, the little Geordie Golfer gave the biggest drubbing ever administered to a field of top Professionals. He spread-eagled the field to emerge the winner by 16 shots with a four-round total of 278 – a cherished record that stood for many years. Tied for second place and completely out of the hunt was Bobby Jones. . . . They had travelled together to Hamilton, Ontario for the tournament. One wonders what the conversation was between them on the way home.

It was a great shock to the golfing world when only two years later, and after further successes Douglas Edgar was dead, aged only 36. No one can say for certain what caused his tragic death for the circumstances are shrouded in mystery. Though it can be said unequivically that his death was very sudden and not of his own doing. On August 9th in the year 1921, at the height of his golfing prowess, he was discovered with blood gushing from a severed femoral artery on the steps of his boarding house in Atlanta. Edgar was found dying by his room-mate and friend, Thomas Wilson. The latter was reported to have said at the time: 'He tried to tell me something, but I couldn't understand. He died before reaching hospital'.

The sudden death of Edgar prompts three theories:

No. 1. Was he struck down and killed by a speeding passing motorist? A Police investigation drew no firm conclusion; the death was entered into the files of the Georgia Police Authorities as 'Possibly caused by an automobile accident'.

No. 2. Was he killed because of his defiance of a gangland threat to 'lose' the Southern 'Open'?

No. 3. Was he killed by a local gang for not taking 'a dive' in the head-to-head match with a golfing opponent in Atlanta, on whom money had been laid, to beat Edgar?

Which theory is the right one? Perhaps no one will ever know though the conscensus of opinion on this side of the Atlantic is that foul play was involved. The family of Edgar did not rule out foul play; they found that the body was not bruised (as it might have been if hit by a speeding car); there were signs of a scuffle in the area of his home; and the wound which killed was only half-an-inch wide, three inches deep, more like a stab-wound than a car injury.

It is time that a proper place in golfing's history is accorded to James Douglas Edgar of Newcastle upon Tyne. His book on golf instruction was a classic of its time, acknowledged as such by master golfers of his era; he was also said to be the man who took the modern golf swing to the United States. His cardinal principle of teaching was hitting from in to out and keeping the right elbow tucked up against the right side until the ball had been played. When he felt 'right', Edgar could play beautiful golf.

Commentators who saw him often used the analogy of the musical genius who could produce breath-taking orchestral performances, manipulating his instruments as he fancied, making them play any tune.

After watching him play, the great Harry Vardon said of Douglas Edgar: 'This is the man who one day will be the greatest of us all'.

THE 'CITY' AND DR. ALISTER MACKENZIE LINK WITH WORLD FAMOUS ARCHITECT DESIGNER OF AUGUSTA NATIONAL

Apart from the 'City's' link with the immortal Bobby Jones through Douglas Edgar, the City of Newcastle G.C. has another link with the course that Jones made famous – Augusta National, home of 'The Masters'. The man who designed that, Dr. Alister Mackenzie, also carried out considerable improvements at the Three Mile Bridge around the time of the Great War.

The Augusta National course, which was not completed until 1934 emerged as an arena of great beauty as well as providing a severe test of golfing skill. Mackenzie and Bobby Jones, who worked closely together on building Augusta turned their project into an art form, and rejected may common concepts of course-building, including large areas of rough and narrow fairways.

We are fortunate in Newcastle that Mackenzie's influence over the 'City' Course in those post-war years was very considerable. He filled in a number of bunkers and built new ones in more strategic positions; he recommended the cutting down of many bushes and reduced the area of rough, all of which held play up. His improvements affected no fewer than 12 out of the 18 holes, and the work was so demanding that 10 extra greens staff were employed for a period of three months.

Dr. Mackenzie told The 'City' Committee that flatness in a golf course was no objection provided that the bunkering was properly done, and the contours were well conceived. He liked to make a golfer think, to have the option to choose between caution and courage, at the same time offering a course that provided enjoyment for the many. With the help of Harry Vardon who laid out the original course at the Three Mile Bridge, Alister Mackenzie succeeded in producing a course on which every single member could enjoy playing, no matter what handicap.

Dr. Mackenzie paid several visits to the 'City' Course, at an economical cost to the 'City' Coffers, according to entries in the Minutes. His fees varied between £5 – £10 plus travelling expenses from his Leeds home. Son of a Scottish Father and English mother, Alister Mackenzie was a keen golfer who abandoned a career in medicine to design golf courses, We are fortunate to have his touch on our own course, for he went on to design some of the finest courses in the world, not least Cypress Point, USA.

Illustrations

Left: Edgar, said to be the man who took the modern golf swing to the United States, was the first to teach 'hitting through the gate' to produce the classic in-to-out swing (demonstrated here in 1920). In the same year, he produced his own instruction book on the modern game, 'The Gate to Golf', said by the great Tommy Armour to be the best of them all.

Right: Pictured on the first tee at 'The Park' in 1914, where he also served as Professional. Edgar was one of golf's straightest hitters: in practice, he liked to drive balls between railway lines to achieve repeated accuracy. After his death, 'The Times' wrote: 'Edgar was a typical North Countryman with strong views . . . but he had all the kindliness which so often goes with a character.'

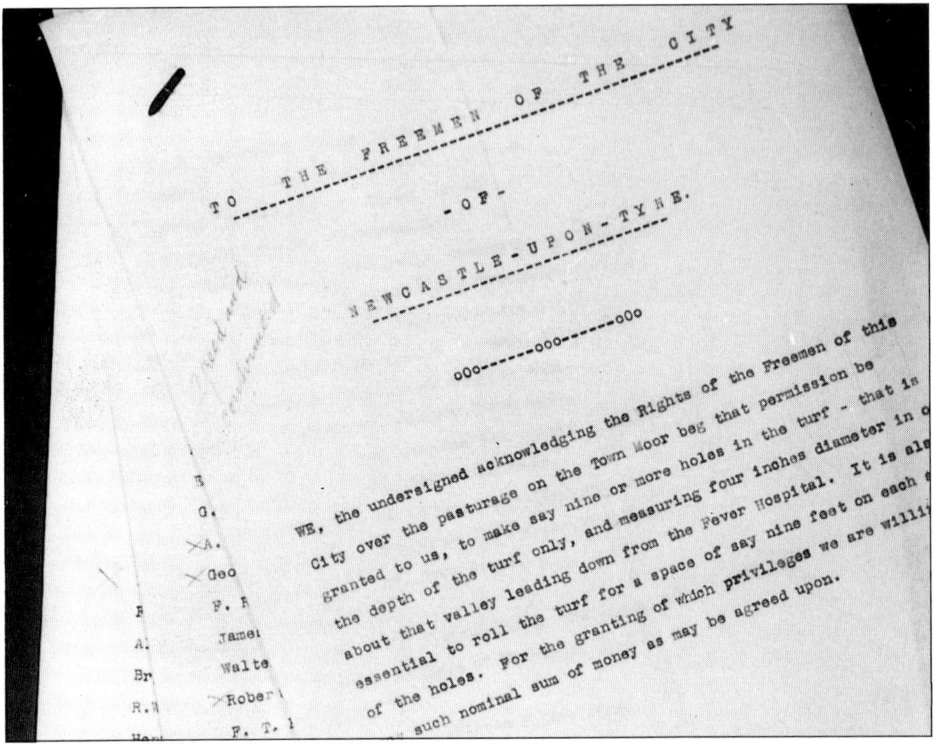

TO THE FREEMEN OF THE CITY

-OF-

NEWCASTLE-UPON-TYNE.

ooo------ooo------ooo

WE, the undersigned acknowledging the Rights of the Freemen of this City over the pasturage on the Town Moor beg that permission be granted to us, to make say nine or more holes in the turf - that is the depth of the turf only, and measuring four inches diameter in c about that valley leading down from the Fever Hospital. It is als essential to roll the turf for a space of say nine feet on each of the holes. For the granting of which privileges we are willi such nominal sum of money as may be agreed upon.

Top: First President, John William Pease driving off the tee-ing ground to open officially the Town Moor course.

Bottom: A copy of the historic petition applying to begin a golf club on the Town Moor, submitted to the Freemen of the City of Newcastle on June 10th, 1891.

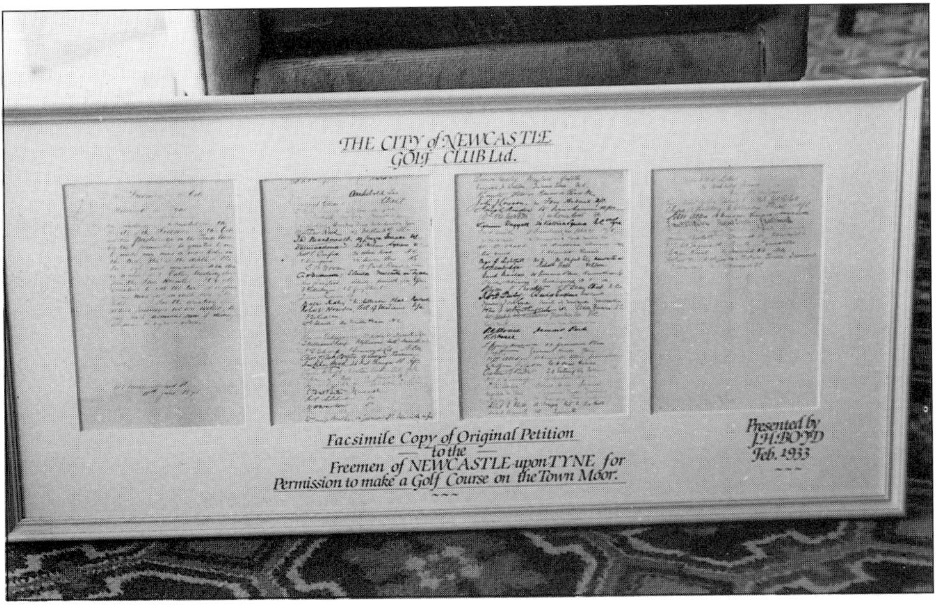

The facsimile reproduction bearing the names of the original signators to the Petition to the Freemen seeking permission to construct a golf course. It was presented to the Club in 1933 by the then Captain, John Boyd (who also served as the club's Hon. Solicitor).

Top: Early golf balls played at 'the City'. The ball named 'The Gutty' on the left was a solid lump of gutta-percha, hardened, painted white and played by members until 1898. The other ball, 'The Haskell' was introduced from America in 1899 and was much superior (its centre tightly wound with fine rubber and covered with vulcanised material).

Bottom: A prized relic on permanent display in the clubhouse: the hickory-shafted wood made by the first 'City' Professional, Tom Fernie and used by the first Club Champion (Beaumont Pease).

Top: At the time of the Great War, golf was confined to the professional classes and the well-to-do. Pictured here is the Captain of 'The City' in 1914, Mr. C. H. Watson with his daughter in the saddle at Woolsington Hall.

Bottom: The unluckiest 'birdie' of all time. The crow that was killed by the first shot played from the first tee on the first day's play at the Three Mile Bridge in August, 1907.

Views of the Chimney Mill, the first clubhouse rented from the Newcastle Brewery Company of W. B. Reid who had used it as a corn mill. Top picture shows the location in Claremont Road looking towards the Haymarket. The bottom photograph is the reverse view.

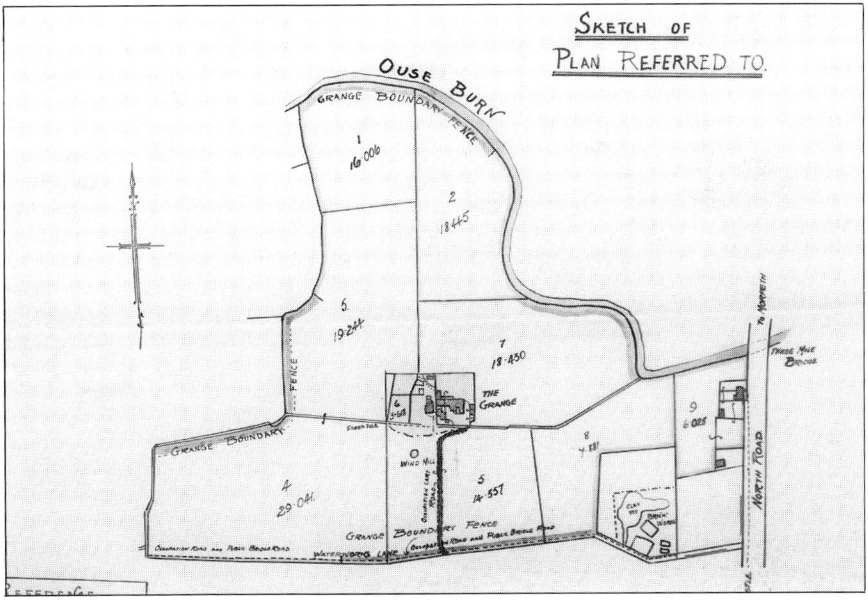

Top shows the picturesque old clubhouse at Three Mile Bridge before the addition of the sun-lounge in the 1920's.

Bottom shows the original 1907 plan for the course lay-out at Three Mile Bridge. Note that the Southern boundary way was known as 'Waterworks Lane'.

Top: Captain's drive-in at 'The City' in 1934 with Professional James Fryer presenting a new ball to the new Captain of the Club, W. B. Taylor.

Bottom: A golfing group of members pictured outside the clubhouse in the 1930's. The Professional (white jacket) is Cyril Fryer. On the back row (third from left) is Cromer Moffat, a county player, who could not have known then that his son, David would win his first County Championship in 1958 at the age of 22.

THIS IS IT—CHAMPIONSHIP HOLE-IN-ONE

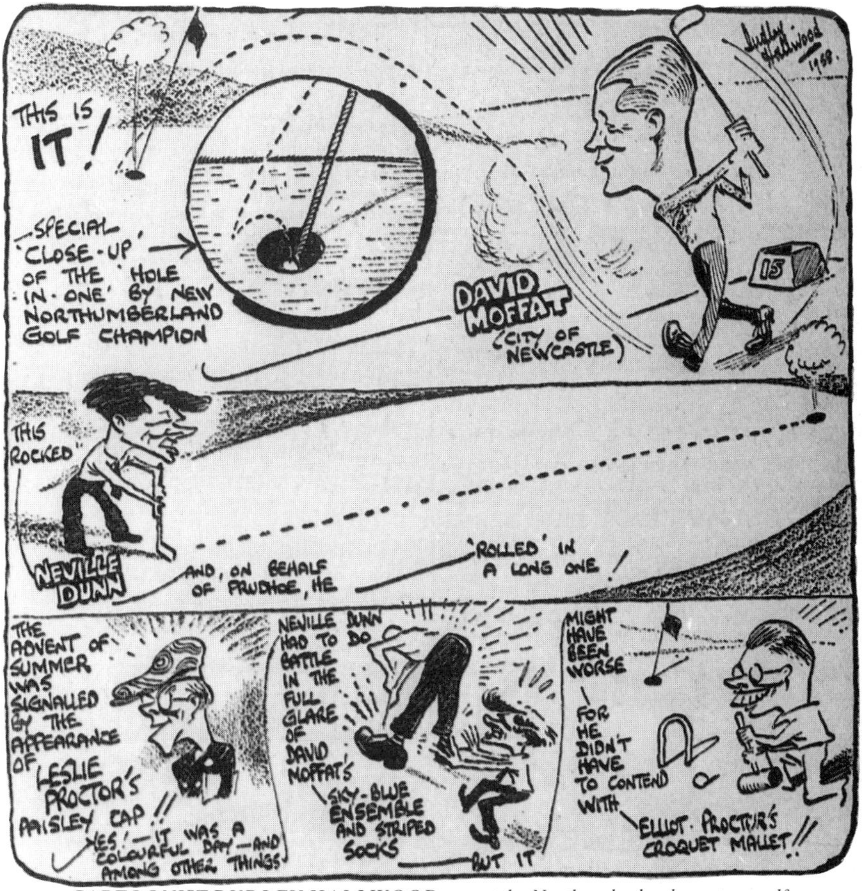

CARTOONIST DUDLEY HALLWOOD was at the Northumberland amateur golf championship final on Saturday.

Hole-in-one David Moffat a worthy champion

DUNN MADE GREAT FIGHT

By LARRY FIGGIS

Moffat won his first County Championship in 1958 in great style, though it took a hole-in-one to close out the losing finalist, Neville Dunn of Prudhoe. (Cartoon by Dudley Hallwood.)

Top: The celebrated footballer and manager of Newcastle United F.C., Joe Harvey was at one time a regular player at 'the City'. From the 1960's, a number of United stars were often seen on the 'City' course, including Bobby Mitchell and Jackie Milburn.

Bottom: This Dudley Hallwood cartoon, showing leading club members and officers, appeared in the 'Evening Chronicle' in July, 1973.

Chapter V

TWENTY-FIVE BUSY YEARS 1914–1939

The outbreak of the great conflict of 1914 was bound to seriously affect the fortunes of the City of Newcastle Club.

The days of playing an enjoyable 18 holes, adjourning to the '19th hole' for a bottle of Bass for 3d or a tot of whisky for 6d followed by a substantial lunch for 1/9d were to be only memories for many. Scores of 'City' golfers joined the Colours and left Newcastle. More than 100 left in the first year of the war, and numbers on active service increased as the years went by. An early casualty was Lt. J. Kent, an ex Capt. The 'City' decided to carry on as best they could. But by 1915 the Army had moved in and trenches had been dug on the course, requiring the introduction of a local rule for general play. Sheep were allowed to graze on a certain area of the course; aircraft action risk insurance was taken out.

Nearly a quarter of the club's membership was in uniform by 1916 and the General Committee decided to waive their subscriptions until the end of the war.

There were many unusual situations to be confronted – such as the request from South Shields Golf Club to play at the Three Mile Bridge as their course had been requisitioned by the Army. The 'City' said 'Yes' and allowed free use of the course.

The 'City' Club started to take a metaphorical battering as the war continued; finances started to fall, ending in an all-time low. In order to raise cash, the Club introduced a Debenture Loan Scheme in 1916 which members responded to. (Though it took six years to pay those loans off.)

By 1917, after three years of the deprivations of war, the stresses and strains began to bite even more deeply. The greens staff was reduced to a minimum and the Professional dismissed, leaving employees being informed that their dismissal was for the duration only. The course was reduced in size from 18 holes to 10.

Even after this fairly drastic action, there was little improvement in the finances of the Club. The result was that the Club had to seek a loan of £500 to keep going, and get the promise of another £600 if required. When the last rifle shot had rung out over the Western Front, and the Allies were celebrating victory after appalling slaughter on both sides, the 'City' stood back and counted the cost.

It was of a very high order. Many 'City' members had been seriously wounded and a considerable number would never return. There was mourning for the men who would not come back from the Flanders Fields.

The Lord Mayor of Newcastle unveiled a Club Memorial to those members killed on active service. This epitaph on a brass shield hung first in the club dining room, later in the hallway.

Although all felt relieved that peace had come at last – and that despite all deprivations, the 'City' had kept going through the war years – members were hardly prepared for the news that the Club was going to close!

What happened was that earlier, and towards the close of the Great War, the then Wartime Agricultural Committee required the Club to plough up 111 acres in order to sow seed. The 'City' appealed and delayed that action. But by 1918 there was a large crop of hay to be harvested on the 'City's' meadows; the club committee decided to close the Club from March 25th until the hay crop was won. By temporarily closing down the Club and suspending the staff, the hay could be gathered in as part of the war effort and at the same time could generate cash for the struggling 'City' Club.

The intensive labour needed for bringing in the harvest was provided by 'City' members who were able to buy club refreshments at half-price for the duration of the work.

As a result of that, coupled with money raised from the members' loan account, the Club was virtually able to wipe out its bank overdraft. The course was closed for three months.

After the end of hostilities, the 'City' Club slowly got back into its stride and returning ex Service-men were a welcome sight on the first tee.

The experience of four years of war against the 'Hun' had left its mark. There is a Club minute, dated January, 1919 which lays down the law for one class of visitor. It states, 'No person of enemy origin shall be allowed to become a member of the Club, and no such person shall be permitted to play on the course'. The author has found no minute in the 'City' records to rescind that. If that is so, then the implications of that ruling are quite staggering, especially in the context of today's international golfing community!

'City' golfers practiced and prepared themselves for the first full competition for years in 1919. By that year, members competed for some half-dozen trophies in all. The seventh trophy was given in the same year by Councillor T. W. Rowe J.P. to commemorate the 'Glorious Victory in the European War 1914–1918'. The 'Rowe Victory Cup' was to be an 18-hole medal handicap, and the donor asked that there should be no entry fee for this competition.

In the following year 'The Captain's Cup' was presented by Mr. E. Fogg, awarded to the player returning the lowest net score on Captain's Day. Also in 1920, the then Lord Mayor of Newcastle, Sir John Fitzgerald presented 'The Fitzgerald Rose Bowl' to be awarded for the annual winner of an 18-hole medal handicap competition.

A few year's later, in 1924, another Lord Mayor of Newcastle, Councillor Stephen Easten gave a handsome cup for Calcutta competition. That was to replace the shield presented in 1895, which it was agreed should hang in the clubhouse, (winners' names of subsequent years to be added on small silver plates). It will be seen from the fore-going that the links between Newcastle Corporation and the Club remained strong.

As the club competitions hotted up, the Greens Committee introduced a rule which started mutterings in the locker room. In future all competition cards were to be returned, whether the course was completed or not. Failure to do so would place the offending member under penalty for the next competition played.

The committee also decided that green fees should be raised. At this time, visitors paid 2/- per day Monday to Friday and 5/- at weekends. A monthly ticket could be bought for £1 and schoolboy sons of members could play for 1/- per day.

Through the years, the 'City' has always been a popular venue with actors and artists golfers who performed in the city's theatres – hence the special entry in the club minutes, 'Theatricals – 5/- per week'.

The years following the first world war were very challenging; not least of the 'City's' problems was repairing war-time damage and bringing all the fairways and greens up to standard. Apart from part of the course being used for grazing cattle, with other areas used to cultivate hay crops, there was the inevitable damage resulting from part-occupation by the military. One entry in the minute books reads: 'Payment for trench damage as per North Command – £19.00'.

The 'City G.C.' managers were far-seeing when it came to making improvements on the course, calling for advice and reports from one of the top golf course experts in the country, Dr. Alister McKenzie.

The professional at this time, Mr. Andrew Kay was warned about taking leave of absence without permission. His services to the Club must have been satisfactory though, as shortly afterwards a minute states, 'That Kay be allowed his meals in the clubhouse free of charge, as it appears to be the custom with other clubs to make this allowance'.

Caddies were very much in use by members after the war, though the eagerness of the caddie boys to learn the rudiments of the game on the 'City' course had to be restrained in the interests of members. One minute of 1919 reads, 'The secretary was requested to bring to the professional's notice that caddie boys were not allowed to play off any tees near the clubhouse, nor for that matter anywhere on the course'. The minutes also record that at this time there had been several losses of property from the locker room. 'The boy employed by Mr. Kay was found to be dishonest. This boy must leave at once.'

In this period following World War I, the wages paid by the 'City' to the greens staff were relatively high: the head greenkeeper (Thomas George Black) received £3 per week, two senior greenkeepers £2 5s per week and the junior 37s 6d per week. As a guide to the reader on comparative prices, in the 1920's one could buy a half pint of beer, a small packet of cigarettes and a box of matches and get change out of sixpence (2½p today).

In those days, before the introduction of wooden pegs, the practice for members was to use sand provided on the tees in order to tee-up their balls for the drive. One Greens Committee minute reads, 'Instructions were to be given that the sand in the tee boxes should be kept moist and the water boxes properly filled. A small amount of rock salt was recommended to be placed in the sand boxes in order to keep the sand moist'.

Although the internal combustion engine had been invented years before, the 'City' greens staff still used horses for pulling gangs as well as the more modern tractor for course work. One minute from 1926 read, 'Purchase of horse, £10; sale of horse £3; purchase of tractor from the Northern Agricultural Company, £216'.

By 1924 the full-playing member at the 'City' was paying an annual subscription of five guineas. But when the committee decided the next year to raise the amount to £6-12s-6d a rumpous blew up in the Club. The members would not have it and threw the proposal out – which caused three committee men to resign on the spot, and the remainder to resign at the end of the year. But despite all the problems, the Club just carried on.

During these post-war years, the 'City' gained a reputation for running a first-class clubhouse that served excellent meals. The Steward was Thomas Ball and his wife, 'Queenie' was a first-class cook. Their son, Tom Ball, now of Powburn Gardens, Fenham, Newcastle upon Tyne lived at the 'City G.C.' with his parents and gave the author a first hand account of what life was like in the late 1920's.

He said that his father was introduced to the 'City' by Major Curtis, a leading light of the 'City' Club who knew Mr. Ball when he ran the officers' mess at a Darlington army base during the war. Mr. Ball signed a contract at the 'City G.C.' for £2 10s per week, and apart from free living quarters he was given several other 'perks'. One of those was to play golf without charge on the 'City' course. Working under the Steward was a staff of four, two of whom (serving maids) also lived in.

Although he was only a young boy, Mr. Tom Ball Junior can recall that the 'City' Clubhouse was run like a royal palace; members did not need to rise to get drinks, maids were on hand. The club restaurant was often full. For the sum of 2s 4d, a three-course meal including roast, sweet and coffee could be taken at leisure. In the month of June, 1919, alone some 1,550 meals were served to members. If you preferred the tasty afternoon tea instead, that would set you back 9d.

In the ten years that Thomas Ball remained as the steward of the Club he became an exceptional golfer. He could play all the shots, became a scratch player, and the only slight suspect part of his game was said to be his putting.

Mr. Cyril Ward, a contemporary golfer who was Newcastle Corporation's Legal Officer told Mr. Ball Junior that his father was the longest hitter he had ever seen. He invariably drove well over 200 yards off the tee, which – in those days – was the equivalent to a good drive from a Professional. He did not believe in carrying many clubs; he had seven or eight at the most in his bag, but was adept at working each club to suit a particular shot. Mr. Ball, an employee, could not take part in 'City' competitions, though in open competition outside the 'City' he won a number of trophies. Members often asked to play with him.

Mr. Ball Junior recalled that the 'City Pro.' in the 1920's was Cyril Fryer, 'a tall, no-nonsense Scot'. He was said to be rather bombastic; and although a useful golfer, his excellence was in teaching the game. He supervised the greens staff and ran the group of caddies at the 'City'.

One crisis that Tom Ball Jnr. recalls at the 'City' was that of 1925 and 'The Big Flood'. There was continuous heavy rain for several days in Newcastle. One morning Mr. Ball awoke, looked down the 18th fairway and could hardly believe his eyes – as far as he could see the 'City' golf course was under water. The 18th fairway and green were completely immersed. He saw the club cat, 'Jimmy' swim out and catch water rats. After leaving the City Golf Club in 1929, Mr. Ball Senior became a well-known Newcastle personality. He accepted a post as the Lord Mayor's Butler and Town Hall Officer, but after some time was promoted to become Superintendent of the Mansion House in Newcastle, becoming well-known to many civic leaders, Newcastle business and professional men. He retired from that post after many years service, and died in 1967 at the age of 78.

It was during the 1920's that the 'City G.C.' was lit properly for the first time. Three 'City' members, Messrs. Andrews, Cairns and Hughes were responsible for the introduction of electric light, a generous gesture indeed as the installation was free. That was in 1925, though the 'City' lights did not burn so brightly the following year when a national confrontation was to occur which was to affect everyone – the General Strike. The North-East was already stricken with high unemployment, a situation worsened by the nationwide strike; the effects of the long slump severely tested the finances of the 'City G.C.' By 1928 the area was still being ravaged by very high unemployment, a state of affairs reflected in the minute books of the 'City'. When the Club advertised for a Steward in 1928, there were more than 200 applications for the job.

Somehow, the Club weathered the storm, though increases in subscriptions were the order of the day.

One event which lifted the gloom for a short time was a special challenge match between one of the star names of the 1920's, Abe Mitchell who took on two of the 'City's' best players, Ernie Sullivan and S. Dempster. The match, sponsored by the 'Daily Express' drew a large crowd which saw the power of the 'Pro' succeed. Sullivan was one of the best-ever golfers to come out of the 'City' – he played off scratch or near scratch for 40 years and won countless competitions in his career. The complete Sullivan story is told later in this book.

A signal honour came to the Club in 1931 when J. Beaumont Pease was elected Captain of the Royal and Ancient Club. In 1936 the Club lost a valued and respected member in Sir Stephen Easten. A former 'City G.C.' President, he had given great service to the Club. As a memorial, an electric clock was installed in the western wall of the clubhouse.

By this time, the Club had placed itself on a firmer financial footing and looked like going from strength to strength as golf gradually grew more popular. By 1939 there were 250 full-playing members; plus a healthy ladies' section; the course was well-kept and an attractive challenge to any golfer. Then the Second World War broke out. . . .

This historic picture shows how Cromer Moffat, playing in an inter-county event of the late 1920's successfully negotiated a 'stymie'.

Chapter VI

TRIALS OF WORLD WAR II AND THE POST WAR YEARS

Only 21 years after the end of the war to end all wars, the City of Newcastle Golf Club was plunged into another long conflict, starting in 1939. By 1941, as the call to the Colours began to drain the Club membership, serious financial problems once more confronted the Club. In October 1939 the Club had successfully negotiated with the landlords to reduce the annual rent of £600.00 to £400.00 for a period of 12 months. At the end of that period a new application made by the Club for the continuance of the reduced rental of £400.00 failed. An appeal to members for financial help proved unsatisfactory. Short of available liquid funds the Club committee met in crisis, when a majority voted to wind the Club up.

It was mainly a fighting rearguard action by the chairman and vice-chairman that saved the day; they persuaded the landlords to arrive at a compromise solution reducing the need to pay the extra sum on the due date. However, it was a very near thing to the complete close-down of the 'City' Club. In the archives is a copy of the official winding-up letter prepared by the secretary and chairman in readiness to dispatch. The letter stated that if and when the Club closed down 'an effort will be made to resuscitate it after the war, with pastures new to play over. . . .'

So golf of a kind went on at the 'City', though it was restricted as part of the land was occupied by the Military, and another section let with grazing rights for £100.00 per annum to a neighbouring farmer called Reay. All Club competitions were cancelled. 'City' members who joined the Armed Forces were granted honorary membership for the duration of the war.

As the conflict dragged on golfing equipment became scarce, and it was impossible to buy new balls, though 'remoulds' could be purchased from the Pro.'s shop.

The records suggest that the 'City' Club was at its height as a golfing force in Northumberland in the pre-1939 and post war years. High on the list of county 'greats' must stand the names of Edgar Gray, Ernie Sullivan and his friend Gilly Boswell. Sullivan was master of the short game and the half-shot winning more than 30 'City' G.C. trophies. Boswell, a true Romany and an outstanding amateur golfer was without question the best-dressed man on the 'City' or any other golf course. His elegance in dress was matched by his classic, graceful swing which won him two 'City' Club Championships just prior to the war. With Cromer Moffat, the father of David Moffat, he also won the coveted 'Chronicle Cup' in 1939. (Inter-County Foursomes).

Ernie Sullivan was supreme in foursome competition and matchplay. The Sullivan-Boswell partnership was a daunting prospect for any opponents; the record books show that they were very rarely beaten. Sullivan's other favourite partner was Edgar Gray, a fine golfer in his own right.

Together, they won the Newcastle 'Chronicle Cup' no less than three times in five years. Later, Edgar Gray took a younger partner called David Moffat, winning the Chronicle Cup for 'City' G.C. for a record seventh time in 1956. Under the rules of this important competition, the 'City' G.C. was allowed to keep the trophy for all time. For years, this large solid silver trophy graced a corner of the clubhouse. Despite the fact that it was chained to the wall, thieves broke into the clubhouse and stole it years ago; unfortunately, it has never been heard of since.

The illustrious careers of Ernie Sullivan, Gilly Boswell, Edgar Gray and David Moffat are described in a later chapter.

The years following the end of the 1939–45 war were of crucial importance to the 'City' Club: for the first time the 'City' managers started to talk about purchasing the golf course. By 1946 it was established that the land on which the course was laid out was not to be used for building purposes; its value would be that of argicultural land, making a buy-out a distinct possibility.

No agreement was reached on purchase and in January, 1947, the Club lease was renewed for three years at an increased rent of £800.00 per year. However, succeeding Club committees kept the matter on the agenda, and on October 25th, 1948, a contract was agreed with the landlord to buy out the compound and car parks facing the Great North Road. The land, measuring some 2.13 acres and including two cottages, cost the 'City' G.C. £2,300.00 – with hindsight, a bargain for a prime site in Gosforth.

Of course the great prize, the ownership of the golf course itself had yet to be won. By the early 1950's the owner, Mrs Bainbridge was agreeable to a sale, and the committee instructed the Hon. Solicitor for the Club to make an offer for the land.

Unfortunately, it is a sorry story to relate which ended in failure. John Boyd, the solicitor who handled the transaction for the Club, critical of the committee's approach, claims that little preparation of the ground was made; no tentative approach was made to the owner to sound out a figure; and the offer from the committee was pitched far too low. According to Mr. Boyd, he was instructed to offer the sum of £9,000 for the many acres of prime land on which the golf course stood. When the owner rejected the offer, no follow up was made. Looking back on the affair, Mr. Boyd said, 'Had it been handled properly I'm sure that we could have done a deal. Instead the owner said 'No' and a great opportunity was lost'.

Although the Club failed in its attempt to buy out the course, one has some sympathy for the committee's guarded approach: in the early 1950's the Club's finances were strained, budgets had been cut. In fact in February, 1951 an extra-ordinary general meeting was called to make an urgent increase in subscriptions, from £8.8.0 to £10.0.0. The secretary, Jim Colpitts, offered to take a cut in salary which was accepted. The golf explosion, which would generate new cash resources was still more than a decade away.

Later, the land on which the course stood would be sold by the Bainbridges to Gosforth Urban Council. Nevertheless, by 1958 the 'City' G.C. Committee again discussed making approaches to buy out the land. By this time, the value of the land had risen to some £25,000.00, a very considerable increase on the first asking price. The position was further complicated by the knowledge that the local Council was planning to seize land on the South side of the course for use by the Education Authority. Once more negotiations came to nothing. . . .

During the Local Government re-organisation in 1974, the land in question passed from Gosforth Council to Newcastle Corporation who are the present landlords. Our lease with them expires in the year 2014.

SOME HAPPENINGS OF THE 1950's

There was a minor diversion in 1951 which related to a member building a wooden bridge from his house over-looking the 18th hole onto the course. The committee ruled that on a day to be agreed, the bridge would be removed for one day to prevent the right of way being established.

Later that year, the Club lost their Club Professional, Jack Armitage who took up a new post with Temple Newsham Golf Club. He was succeeded by E. J. Wallis who was appointed from the Brighton and Hove G.C.

At about this time, the game of darts was played for the first time in the men's bar; it became so popular that the 'City' formed a team and competed in the local Darts League.

The year, 1957, marked an auspicious year for the City of Newcastle Club – it was exactly 50 years since the Club opened its doors at the Three Mile Bridge. The celebrations included the staging of a special four-ball medal play competition, followed by a dance in the clubhouse. The only sobering thought during that year was another report about ailing finances. The Club President reported a difficult year to which reduced receipts, increased maintenance and running costs had contributed.

May, 1957 marked the retirement from active Club work of one of the Club's most loyal servants and a great character, 'Tot' Colpitts. Many a fledgling member of the 'City' had reason to be grateful for the help and guidance given by this Club secretary.

'Tot' Colpitts, the giver of the greatest service to the City of Newcastle Golf Club over many years, not to mention his years as Club Secretary.

Four 'City' stalwarts with more than 150 years membership and golf between them. L. to R: John Scott, Harold Sharpley and Archie Rutherford. Standing: Bill Foster.

On his retirement day he was heartily commended by the Club chairman for services rendered over many years. Indeed it was a sad day for the 'City' when this grand old gentleman of golf, with a knowledge second to none, eventually disappeared from the Club scene.

The Club was very fortunate to benefit from equally loyal service from his brother, Jim Colpitts, another great servant of the City of Newcastle Club. Jimmy Colpitts was Secretary of the 'City' G.C. for 17 years, including the difficult post-war period and into the challenging 1950's. He contributed immensely to the success of the Northumberland and Durham Alliance of which he was also secretary and organiser for many years.

Like his brother, Jimmy Colpitts was the epitome of the English golfing gentleman on and off the course. Apart from his extensive knowledge of the game, to say nothing of the book of rules, his help was always pleasingly available to all. He was 80 years old when he died in 1972. Before his death, he had left a request that following his cremation his remains be scattered over the 'City' golf course where he had spent so many happy years. Of the two brothers, 'Tot' was the better golfer and always a single figure man.

Mention has already been made of the drastic changes made in the course lay-out in the early 1960's, following acquisition of a section of the course to the South by the local Education Authority.

The course we play on today stems from that re-designed lay-out of 1963, a rather longer course than before with a par of 72 and SSS of 71 at that time.

It was during the mid-sixties that more and more people became interested in taking up the game, some of them fired by the exploits of some of the modern golfing 'greats' as seen live on Television. . . .

Chapter VII

EVENTS LEADING TO THE GOLF EXPLOSION AT THE 'CITY'

By the end of the 1950's and the beginning of the 1960's there was no ominous sign to indicate that by the late sixties a golf explosion would take place – and the 'City G.C.' for the first time would introduce a waiting list for membership.

In fact in May, 1959 the Club was informed that the 'City' books were showing a loss and there was a fall in membership. By 1965 the 'subs.' were again increased, this time by the then considerable sum of £5-5s-0d to £18-18s-0d. The loss in that year was said to be £700.

During these difficult years, the committee of the day discussed and floated various schemes of development in order to raise finance. One of them proposed moving the clubhouse site elsewhere, and building some 60 flats on the large compound fronting onto the Great North Road. . . . For various reasons, none of the schemes came into fruition.

One piece of news to burst on the 'City' scene in July, 1966 was received with not a little shock – Gosforth Council informed the Club that the Ministry of Transport was planning to build a slip road through the Club car park! Hurried meetings were held and protests were made, in view of the fact that the car park would be considerably reduced in size. As time passed, nothing happened; then the 'City' was informed by the Transport Ministry that the road would not be built for 10 years. In the event, the plan was never implemented. . . .

There was some good news in 1966 – for the first time the City of Newcastle G.C. became champions of the Newcastle and District Golf League. The League had been formed in 1951 and competition was always very keen.

Following the end of World War II, 'City G.C.' players applied themselves to the game with earnest dedication, reflected in the honours won on the county scene. By the 1960's, the 'City GC' had carried off numerous County Events, both team and single victories. The evidence is to be found by reading the 'Honours Board' at the end of this book.

By 1964 David Moffat, playing off a plus handicap was already an English International, Northumberland County Champion – and in that year he made 'City G.C.' and golfing history by becoming the first local player to win a national stroke-play event: Sunningdale's Illustrated Gold Vase. (David's golfing triumphs are told in full later in this book).

Other fine 'City G.C.' players who were still going strong included Edgar Gray, four time County Champion and one of the finest iron players ever in the Newcastle area; Harry Hindmarsh, winner of several County Club Championships, and in the 1950's winner of the 'City G.C.' Club Championship three times in four years.

Another fine golfer and affectionately known at the 'City' as 'The New Clubs Specialist' was Arthur Black. He earned the title by starting every season with a brand new set of clubs. He always wanted to play the latest model, and his low handicap testified to his success.

Arthur Black holds one 'City G.C.' record which is unlikely to be ever beaten – in 20 years golf, he holed in one no fewer than 7 times. In addition, he recorded four other 'Aces' at other local courses, giving him a career total of 11 holes in one! He is one of the few golfers who holed 1 so often that he stopped celebrating it. In 1955 when he was 54 years old he holed in 1 at the 'City G.C.' twice in one day. This unusual feat took place at the old 15th short hole (now playing as the 14th).

Tommy Jordan also entered the record books for shooting holes in 1. After joining the 'City G.C.' in 1957, Tommy registered five 'Aces' at his home club in ensuing years, plus another at Alnmouth G.C. (the par 3, 11th hole). In April, 1991, Pat Pepper holed in 1 for the sixth time.

Other 'City G.C.' personalities in the 1960's included Geoff Gill (playing off 2 handicap), John Duncan and Fred Cowley (3 handicap) as well as Bob Jackson and Alan Duncan, both low handicap men.

If there was plenty of confidence shown on the 'City' course, it took until 1966 for the same confidence to be shown about the Club's finances. In that year, members were told at the annual general meeting that the Club now showed a profit – some £700.00 – the best profit to accrue for many years. It was the beginning of the the golf explosion all over the country. As both young men and adults were seized with the golfing bug, the 'City' on October 13th 1969 elected to close the membership for the first time. Membership stood at:

Full playing men – 357

Full playing ladies – 96

Juniors and Social Members were not listed.

During the sixties, two members were honoured by the Club. In August, 1963 David Moffat was elected an Honorary Member of the City of Newcastle G.C. after winning the Northumberland County Stroke Play Championship 'and in view of his previous achievements on the golf course'.

Similarly honoured in January, 1967 was Harold Sharpley, a revered member of the Club who joined the 'City' in 1926.

As the Club moved into the 1970's, two major objectives were on the drawing board – the installation of a 'Pop-up Sprinkler System' and the construction of a new locker room. It says much for the zest and hard work put in by the then committees that both were achieved.

Perhaps the installation of water on the greens was the higher priority. The train of events was that in 1973 the Greens Committee were made aware that a complete new pipe system would have to be installed on the course (the last installation being in 1948). Taking the initiative, Chairman Rod McKenzie (now deceased) discovered that a 'Pop-up System' could be installed for an extra £4,000. So for a total of some £8,000 the 'City' Course benefited from new pipe system plus a brand new sprinkler system. (Imagine the high cost of a new sprinkler system today!)

That piece of enterprise paid for itself in a comparatively short time in savings in staff wages. The traditional method of watering greens, with greens staff spending many hours on each green, was done away with. Another spin-off was the saving of the cost of the water rate, by more efficient control of watering from a console housed in a small room near the clubhouse.

The construction of a new locker room in the early 1970's, though rather overdue was something of a delight for 'City G.C.' members. Spacious, light and tile-carpeted this newly re-furbished room offered large, well-appointed lockers made from high quality timber.

It was said at the time that this new room offered more lockers for playing members than many of the leading clubs in the area – a facility that has been maintained in the new building. Minutes show that the House Committee of the day was commended for its enterprise. Tommy Jordan, who assisted the supervision of the installation work, and numbered all the lockers himself, received special thanks from the club committee.

In 1972 another 'City' stalwart, Tom Percy stepped down from office after many years work on club committees. His wife, Norah, who joined the club with her husband held office in the Ladies Section and did much work for the Club.

The Club minutes of that year record that Archie Rutherford, Club President in 1968 presented a new 'City G.C.' Flag, to be flown on competition days. Archie will be remembered as a keen golfer, a good companion with a genial character. Although he never talked about it, Archie had an outstanding World War I record, for which he was decorated.

Also in 1972, Freddie McNaughton, a member of the 'City G.C.' for many years holed in one playing in a Brancepeth event. Like his late brother, Lennie McNaughton, Freddie has been a fine golfer for decades. Another 'City G.C.' character, the late Jack Kendrick holed his first 'Ace' at the 'City's' 14th during the same year. He had waited 40 years to do it.

After the sudden death on the course of Jack Kendrick in 1973, his widow, Joan presented to the Club the 'Kendrick Salver' for open competition among junior golfers.

The hard-working Captain in 1972, Bill Balfour let little escape his attention. During a busy year, he commended the work of the Ladies Section and particularly their work for the Captain's Wine and Cheese event. Although this old tradition disappeared in recent years, 'City' Lady Members earned a reputation for producing an outstanding table. Older male members who called in at the club on the afternoon preceding the event will recall a great army of ladies beavering away at massive production tables of eatables.

It is with some regret that the author records the demise of one of the old traditional annual matches at the 'City' Golf Club, England versus Scotland. The clash, always hard fought was at the same time played in great spirit; and there was no absence of wit and humour.

Occasionally, after a defeat the Scots had been known to accuse the English of bending the rules! On one occasion, years ago, the English team was charged with sliding in a fine Welsh player in quest for victory!

Though the intensity of the annual battle did not reach a climax until 1973, when, following a rather heavy Scottish defeat, the Scottish Captain was driven to reaching for the pen (rather than the sword) to smite the English down. This work, entitled 'SCOTS WHA HAE' was published first in the Autumn edition of the 1973 'City News'. The author was the skipper of the Scottish Team for a number of years, Jim Browning, who is also a past Captain of the 'City G.C.'

SCOTS WHA HAE!

One sunny day, the Sabbath too
Assembled was a motley crew
Of Scots and English to contest
A battle on this day of rest.

The English by a Renegade
Were led – his plans in secret made
With traitor's heart but friendly face
To 'con' the Scots team to disgrace.

The battle raged for many an hour
With skill, and craft and brutal power
The Scots with open friendly smile
Faced by the cunning English guile.

But on that day, no justice reigned
Satan, the Sassenachs sustained
As balls through bunkers bounced and rolled
The Scots dismayed – their ill-luck tholed.

Against inspired and cunning stuff
Their honest faith was not enough
True to their land of mount and heather
They fought – but perished there together

Another Flodden!! Nay 'tis true
They fought with all the arts they knew
The blood-soaked course was witness mute
The price they paid – one can't compute.

And so the summer air was rent
The pipes and pibrochs did lament
But this was over in a trice
They swallowed hard, but paid the price.

And now the fiery cross began
And will be passed from Clan to Clan
No faint hearts – no future fear
The Sassenachs will pay next year. . . .

by Jim Browning

Chapter VIII

THE TROPHIES – THE 'CITY' AND COUNTY. A HISTORY.

The City of Newcastle Golf Club possesses an outstanding collection of trophies built up over a period of 100 years.

At county level, the 'City' virtually dominated two events for some 40 years, this golden era ending in the late 1960's. The Northumberland–Durham Inter-County Foursomes (the 'Chronicle Cup') was first won in 1929; by 1956, when the Club had been victorious 7 times, the Cup was won outright.

This large, solid silver trophy occupied pride of place in the 'City' clubhouse for many years until one day it was removed by a thief in broad day-light.

The 'Chronicle Cup' had originally been presented by the proprietors of the Newcastle Chronicle and Journal Ltd. After the 'City' won it outright, a new Challenge Cup was presented for competition by Allan Harrison. The 'City' won that trophy in 1959 and 1965, making them winners 9 times of the Inter-County Foursomes. In addition, the Club were losing finalists on another 4 occasions.

The City of Newcastle G.C. has been equally successful in the County Club Teams Championship, winning 9 times in all between 1911 and 1958.

Since the inception of the Northumberland County Championship in 1907, the 'City' has recorded 13 victories in all, though David Moffat (five) and Edgar Gray (four) accounted for most of those.

J. Beaumont Pease, an outstanding golfer who became an English International played out of both the 'City' and Alnmouth.

The first club trophy presented to the 'City' was a gold medal given by J. W. Pease (Father of J. Beaumont Pease) in 1892. In those days the Pease Medal was played as a scratch competition over 18 holes. The inaugural winner was none other than J. B. Pease.

Following the presentation of The Pease Coronation Cup in 1902, the Pease Medal has been awarded for the best scratch score in the first round of that event. The Coronation Cup was given by J. Beaumont Pease to mark the Coronation of Edward the Seventh, and is a 36-hole medal handicap.

The Reid Vase is an historic trophy as it was presented by the well-known Newcastle Brewer, W. B. Reid, the owner of the old windmill in Claremont Road which was converted into the 'City's' first clubhouse. The first winner was H. P. Bailey returning an 81 nett.

For sheer magnificence, the large Calcutta Shield, made of silver with fine etchings of the windmill clubhouse takes some beating. Introduced in 1895, the shield was presented to the winner of a competition decided by match-play on handicap terms.

The Calcutta Shield was 'retired' in 1924 when there was no more room to append winners' names. The new Calcutta Cup was presented by a former Lord Mayor of Newcastle who also became President of the 'City' Club, Sir Stephen Easten.

Top: The table groans under the weight of the 'city' silver. A 100 year history mirrored by this outstanding collection of golf trophies.

Bottom: Past Captains pictured on the 'drive-in' day of 1990–91 Captain, Jack Spencer.
Front, L. to R: Arthur Smith, Norman Finkle, Jack Spencer, Eric Mason and Michael Wilkes.
Second row: Brian Goldwater, Jim Slater, Norman Atkinson and Bill Smith.
Back row: Jim Browning, Norman Dodds, John Sleight, Wilson McAndrew, Jim Cairns, Ken Fish and John Duncan.

When J. B. Garland presented the Garland Cup in 1901 it was for 'Bogey' competition; today it is presented to the winner of an 18-hole par (handicap) competition.

The impact made by the Pease family on the game of golf at the 'City' is reflected by the presentation of yet another trophy by the Peases. The Pendower Medal – presented by J. Beaumont Pease – takes its name from one of the former homes of the Pease Family, Pendower Hall of Newcastle. The best scratch score over 18-holes wins the medal.

No further trophies were presented to the Club for a considerable number of years, hardly surprising with the coming of the Great War. It was fitting, though that a victory trophy should be given to the Club after the cessation of hostilities. Called 'The Rowe Victory Cup' it was presented by Coun. T. W. Rowe to commemorate the 'Glorious Victory in the European War, 1914–1918'. It is played today as a 18-hole medal handicap.

Two trophies were donated in 1920: the Captain's Cup, presented by Mr. E. Fogg and awarded to the player returning the lowest net score on Captain's Day; and the Fitzgerald Rose Bowl, presented by the Lord Mayor of Newcastle, Sir John Fitzgerald and played as a 18-hole medal handicap.

The long winter months are relieved by playing for the Oliver Trophies; despite often bad weather conditions, the competition continues to be intense. Presented by Mr. J. Oliver in memory of his son, Hugh, in 1932 the competition is played via monthly heats with the winners of the six heats qualifying for the final.

When the Turnbull Trophy was presented by Mr. E. Turnbull in 1934, the stipulation was that it should be played as a 18-hole medal handicap on a Wednesday.

In 1936, the first competition to take account of age was introduced into the club fixtures. Mr. Joseph Ellis presented the Gordon Ellis Salver in memory of his son. An 18-hole medal, entry was restricted to members aged 55 and over.

The Joseph Miller Trophy took the place of the Royal Victoria Infirmary Cup Competition (an open competition) which was discontinued in the middle of the 1930's. Perhaps surprisingly, this trophy was donated by a member of a different club. Joseph Miller was a great character and outstanding member of the Northumberland Golf Club. His election to the Presidency of the Northumberland Union of Golf Clubs in 1934 coincided with the demise of the Infirmary Cup event; he then graciously presented the 'City' with a new trophy as traditionally the Infirmary competition had been held at Three Mile Bridge.

The year 1938 saw the introduction of the President's Salver, awarded to the player returning the lowest net score on President's Day.

A competition that always produces the best from golfing partnerships is that for the Collings Trophies. Presented by J. D. Collings in 1951, players compete in a pairs greensome matchplay event.

When Malcolm Smith decided to present a trophy in 1955, the idea was to stimulate competitive golf among higher handicap men. Members of 15 handicap and over qualify over 18 holes medal terms to enter match-play (the top 16 players only) for the 'MacSmith'.

A very popular competition every year is for the George Sinclair Trophy: the first 16 of a medal round qualify for match-play and entrance is limited to members 14 handicap and under.

One of the busiest days of the summer calendar has always been Invitation Day, though it was not until 1964 that two members gave birth to the idea of providing trophies for the winners. The very attractive Rose Bowls were presented by the late Sydney Forster and T. S. Mason.

One of the most revered members of the club throughout its long history was Tot Colpitts. In 1965 the late Gordon Elliott and Ken Potts presented the Tot Colpitts Trophy, to take the form of an 18-hole Stableford Handicap competition.

Another good servant of the club was Tom Bramwell, and in 1965 Pat Bramwell donated 'The Tom Bramwell Trophy' in memory of her father. The present trophy, which replaces the original which was stolen, is given to the winner of a 18-hole medal handicap.

Another stalwart of the club, William Hilton is remembered every year when the 'William Hilton Salver' is played for. It was given in 1968 and takes the form of a 18-hole Stableford.

The best golfers in the club were given the opportunity to come into their own when Gordon Elliott presented a trophy with them in mind in 1975. 'The Gordon Elliott Tankard' is played over 18-holes off scratch.

For the first time, in 1987 the Past-Captains of the City of Newcastle G.C. competed for a trophy in their annual fixture. Presented by John Sleight (Captain 1977), the Cup for Captains is played as a 18-hole competition on Stableford terms.

Returning to further honours won by the 'City' at County level, record books show that the Northumberland County Handicap event often fell victim to the Club. Between 1908 and 1961 'City' players were victorious on no less than 12 occasions. After this event was replaced by the County Salver in 1962, the 'City' won again in 1972 (Andrew McKinna). Eighteen years later, the 'City' repeated the win (Ben Clark). The 'City' has not been as successful in that very old County Handicap Competition, the Forster Cup, though five 'City' players have their names engraved on the cup: H. I. Higginbottom (1932), W. A. Walmsley (1935), Les Potts (1957), Ben Clark (1972) and W. Kitching (1975).

It is worth noting that Ben Clark became the first golfer in Northumberland to win both the Forster Cup and the County Salver.

Chapter IX

THE DAVID MOFFAT STORY

Winner of International and County Honours

Five Times Northumberland Champion

In 100 years of golf at the City of Newcastle G.C. the finest player produced by the Club is David Moffat. His outstanding record reads: boy international, youth international, then full English international; first Northumberland player to win a national stroke play event (The Sunningdale Gold Vase); and County Chamption five times, including three victories from three starts.

At club level, his trophy wins are too numerous to mention – save to say that to date he has won the Club Championship eight times. When he won that championship once again in 1987, it was just 33 years after his first success in that event.

In his hey-day, from the late fifties to the seventies, he became one of the best amateur golfers in the country, an achievement reflected in his frequent selection for England. David was also a member of that outstanding team that became such a force in county golf, affectionately known as 'The Big Six'.

His golfing career began that day in 1947 when he first swung a (cut-down) club at the age of 11 on the old Benton Park course. From the beginning the game fascinated him, and he was fortunate to have a father who himself was a very good golfer. Alexander Cromer Moffat began his golfing career at Benton Park before joining the City of Newcastle G.C.; he was a scratch player who represented Northumberland County.

When David arrived at the Three Mile Bridge Club as a teenager, he soon made his presence felt. At the age of 15 in December, 1951 he drove off the first tee to mark his first card for handicap purposes. He returned a 76 gross which gave him a 'City' handicap of 8.

'City' stalwarts like 'Tot' Colpitts and his brother Jimmy (Club Secretary) were aware that here was a youth of extraordinary talent. Taking him under their wing, they gave him valuable counsel in his formative years. David says that he has never forgotten their words of wisdom.

It was also during 1951 that David, just 15 took the challenging step of proving himself against some of the best junior golfers in Britain, entering the Boys Championship for the 'Carris Trophy'. Many of the competitors were so much bigger and older than Moffat that the Press dubbed him 'The Little Wonder'. He earned that tag because at the end of the final round he only missed victory by 1 shot, playing the difficult closing two holes at Moor Park in 3, 3, in a storming finish.

In the same event the following year – held at Formby – David was drawn to play a towering American, Roger Marks from Del Rio, California, who stood 6 feet and 4 inches tall.

Top: David Moffat holds the Northumberland Championship Trophy in 1969 after defeating Peter Davidson in the final.

Bottom: Moffat receives the President's Bowl after winning the County 72-hole Championship in its inaugural year of 1963. David won this trophy three times. Making the presentation is Charles Storey.

Top: Only 20 years old, Moffat reaches the final of the County Championship played at the Northumberland Club in 1956. After a ding-dong struggle he had to yield to the better player on the day, Gordon Clark of Whitley Bay.

Bottom: In all, David won the County Championship five times. Here seen driving off the first tee at 'The City' in 1969, the start of another successful championship bid.

Moffat not only defeated Marks with an electrifying 4, 4, 4, finish in near gale-force winds, but fought his way through to the fourth round of the tournament. The golf correspondents of both 'The Times' and the 'Daily Telegraph' commended Moffat for the manner in which he handled the difficult course during a gale.

Although this 'City' youth was not yet 20, one feature was emerging in his play that was to stay with him for years to come – the ability to move up a gear and turn on the heat in the final stages of a match. At club level, David was only 16 when he won his first Captain's Prize in 1952 shooting a gross 74.

Another win that year was the 'Bogey Foursomes' at the 'City' with that excellent player, Gilly Boswell who was a power at local and county level for many years. David struck up a golfing empathy with Boswell (whom he called 'Uncle') as well as with another outstanding 'City' player, Edgar Gray (Probably the Club's finest golfer after Moffat. Gray won the County Championship four times and countless club trophies).

If one adds the name of Cromer Moffat to those two, then it is plain that David Moffat surrounded himself with a knowledgeable and powerful golfing triumverate.

The record of the 'clan' Moffat would be incomplete without the achievements of Cromer Moffat. Head of a long-established clothing business in Newcastle's Eldon Square, he first played for Northumberland in 1926 and continued to do so for the next ten years or so, making more than 25 appearances for the county. A check through the records show that A. C. Moffat won many more matches than he lost.

Beginning his golf career at Benton Park, he won the Northumberland and Durham Inter-County Foursomes for the 'Chronicle Cup' with Bill Henderson in 1927. Then joining the 'City' in the early 1930's, and maintaining his county form he won the 'Chronicle Cup' for the second time with Gilly Boswell. In that nail-biting finish at Brancepeth Castle, the 'City' players won on the last green. So the young Moffat was able to learn a thing or two from his father, for whom he had the greatest respect and admiration.

Though it has to be said that David devoted much time and energy to improving himself. Not just the countless hours on the practice ground, but thinking through his game in analytical terms. From early days he kept his scores, sometimes converting them into graph-analysis and penning any observation of faults in play. By being brutally honest with himself, he was able to work on key areas of his game. Thumbing through his scrap books for these early years one could find an entry marked 'County Championship 1953': 'Failed to qualify. I should have done but I will next year. Played badly all day, out of bounds twice and 3 putted four times in 36 holes'. Even so, young Moffat missed the qualification mark by two shots.

In his late teens, David Moffat was already a very stylish golfer with a professional looking swing, an asset commented on by respected Fleet Street golfing correspondents. Little wonder that he was a boy international in 1954 and a youth international in 1955. When he was only 20 he reached the final of the Northumberland County Championship, coming up against another formidable performer by the name of Gordon Clark (Whitley Bay). There was a nice parental touch on the morning of the final; coming down to breakfast, David found a message left by his father before he departed for the office. The little white card said, 'Dear David. Good Luck. Head Down, stay down, put them down and fight like Hell!'

In David's scrap book, alongside the card is: 'This piece of paper means more to me than any other in the book. Dad left it on the breakfast table before I played Gordon'. As it happened, Clark was too good for David that day in 1956 at the Northumberland Golf Club. In fact, Clark struck something of a purple patch in the closing stages, though Press reports of that final say that 'Moffat fought like a tiger and never gave up'.

As Moffat 'became of age' in 1957 he celebrated by being chosen as a youth international. Selected again in 1958 he was appointed Captain of the English team. The late fifties saw David emerge as an irrestible force in Northumberland golf with a hat-trick of wins for the George Renwick Medal in 1955, 56 and 57; and then with 3 wins from 3 starts in the Northumberland County Championship in 1958, 1959 and 1961 (In 1960 he was at St. Andrews playing in the qualifying round of the Open Championship.)

During this period, Moffat was playing some of the best golf of his career, was always the one the others had to beat, and could be said to be one of the finest golfers in the North. It was about this time that he had the misfortune to be involved in a serious accident which was to leave him with a back injury. Though he made a good recovery and returned to golf to win honours at both international and county level, David feels that the injury left its mark.

There was something of a sensation in the Northumberland Championship final of 1958 when David's opponent was Neville Dunn (Prudhoe). The battle was hard-fought and at one of the closing short holes, the 'City' player seized the chance to record his first hole in 1 – as it turned out a crucial blow as it enabled Moffat to defeat Dunn by one hole.

Just four years before in a non-competitive round at the 'City' though all putts were holed and the card was marked by John Duncan, David shot a gross 65 playing off 4 handicap. This astonishing round for a teenager included six birdies and one eagle.

At about the same time, Moffat 'beat' one of the all-time greats of the game – Ben Hogan. After winning the 'Open' at Carnoustie in 1953 Hogan, supported by the British Golf Foundation, threw out a challege to Britain's young golfers. On a selected day, he would play a challenging American course (in the event, Fort Worth G.C.) and back his score against all comers playing a medal round at their own course off handicap. Playing off plus 2, Hogan went round Fort Worth in par figures (72) giving him a return of 74 (72 plus 2). Moffat, off 4 handicap shot a nett 71, beating Hogan by 3 strokes and receiving a signed Certificate from Hogan to that effect.

By the time he reached his early twenties, David was able to study his personal records, updated annually, to follow his scores and rounds for the year. His first entry in his record book, in 1952 when he was 16 shows that over 41 competitive rounds he averaged 78.9 gross score. Four years later, his gross average had reduced to 75.5 and he bettered that within the next few years.

David Moffat, with the 18th green and flag of the 'City' behind him, pictured in Centenary Year.

As well as working on his game, David devoted time to keeping fit with regular visits to the gymnasium. The effort was rewarding. The 'little boy golfer' who played in 'the Carris' in 1951 was a more powerful looking player in his twenties. In the early sixties, one golf correspondent referred to Moffat 'as a broad-shouldered young man, 5ft 10½ins tall and 12st 7lb in weight.'

One of David's biggest scalps was that of the Walker Cup star, Michael Lunt in the English Championship at Formby in 1958. Once more, the 'City' player demonstrated his ability to turn it on in the closing stages, ending the match with an electrifying finish of three 3's. The 'Times' golf correspondent wrote: 'Moffat's swing has the smooth acceleration of the better professionals, and his control of all shots in the wind was impressive.'

Another golf correspondent, welcoming the news that selectors were trying to instil the killer instinct into British teams, advised them to look no further than Moffat. The journalist reported: 'David Moffat has that instinct. He plays to win, and win easily if possible'.

About this time Moffat, in his early twenties and making his mark in top amateur golf was accused by some of 'being an exhibitionist on the course'. Those critics, though few in number, brought down the wrath of the Newcastle golf correspondent, Larry Figgis, who called the criticism, 'sour grapes'.

'Exhibitionism is a common outlet for genius in golf or anything else' wrote Figgis in the 'Newcastle Journal', 'Nobody criticised Walter Hagen in his hey-day, and he was probably the greatest showman of them all. I am not suggesting that Moffat is a Hagen but I am tired of hearing him criticised by people who did not even know him. He is the best amateur golfer in the North-East – and he has not reached his peak yet – so let us give credit where credit is due'. That comment was penned in August, 1959 when David was 23 years old. Many who have played golf with David Moffat over the years, far from accusing him of anything, would point to him as an example of model behaviour on a golf course.

During that same year, Moffat answered his critics by an outstanding display of golf to win that very tough event, the Northumberland and Durham Open. Catching fire at Seaton Carew Course in the closing stages, Moffat shot 2, 3, 4, 3, for the last four holes of that testing circuit to defeat Bert Gadd of Bishop Auckland by 3 shots.

The decade of the 1960's was a happy and rewarding one for David when he won many honours as a European and International player, as well as numerous Club honours. Strangely enough, one of his biggest single wins was somewhat marred by the experience of a friend playing in the same tournament, the Sunningdale Gold Vase. The unhappy story involved his fellow Northumbrian, Alan Thirlwell who was playing behind him in the final round. Coming to the last two holes, Thirlwell seemed to have the field well-beaten with shots in hand. Incredibly, he took 12 for the last two holes to lose the tournament by one shot to David.

Looking back on his long and incident-packed career, Moffat names two other golfers he loved to have as a partner, Edgar Gray of the 'City' and Gordon Clark of Whitley Bay. David treasures his times with Gray who took him under his wing as a youth, imparting sound golfing knowledge. Indeed the Gray-Moffat partnership was a formidable one at all levels of golf.

Gordon Clark was the best kind of partner one could have, especially in tough county competition. 'I loved playing with him and Gordon was never beaten, no matter what the state of the game' said Moffat.

David's achievements in golf competition over a period of many years are quite outstanding. Apart from his five wins in the Northumberland Championship starting in 1958, he has won the Northumberland and Durham Open three times, and the Northumberland 72-Hole Stroke Play Championship twice. He was an English Boys Selector in the 1980's, Northumberland Captain in 1977 and again in 1985–86. He played for his country as a boy international, from 1955 as a youth, and from 1961–67 as a full international. (The full record of honours are listed at the back of the book.)

Exactly 40 years ago, David came to the City as a boy of 15. Now in his mid-fifties he has forged a permanent link with the Club. He, perhaps more than anyone is conscious of the achievements and great traditions of the City of Newcastle Golf Club. A Club that over the years has produced many fine players, characters and upholders of all that is best in the game of golf.

He acknowledges with pride the association and help he has received through the years by men from the 'City'. People like Edgar Gray, Gilly Boswell, Bill Hilton, 'Tot' and Jimmy Colpitts, George Cairns, Moss Rutherford, Arthur Black, Norman Duncan, Jim Ferris, Tommy Meikle and Ken Fish, to name but a few.

'I have wonderful memories of golf at the "City" ' said David 'What is amazing is that I can remember details of matches that took place years ago, even shots played in a round. Even today I can walk up to a spot on the course and mark within a yard where a vital shot was played during an important match'.

If David Moffat has indelible memories of golf at the 'City', the Club reflects in the glory that his achievements on golf's greens and fairways have brought to our name. Those who are fortunate to have witnessed 'Moff' in his hey-day – catching fire and off on another electrifying charge – will know that they have seen something special. One is left with a tantalizing thought: 'What glittering prizes might there have been had he turned professional?' After all, from an early age, his golfing icon was a man called Hogan. . . .

Chapter X

THE 'CITY' FORGES AHEAD

Major Developments Launched

During the 1970's there was much discussion about the lack of facilities in the clubhouse. The argument was that a Club the calibre of the City of Newcastle G.C. deserved a separate dining-room; expansion to allow larger functions to be accommodated; a separate area for games; and better bar facilities.

The catalyst for this first major improvement was chairman Norman Finkle. In 1979 he brough before members a development plan estimated to cost some £80,000.

The idea was to secure a loan from the Federated Breweries to finance the project. Unfortunately, after the decision was approved, the national economy worsened, credit became scarcer, and the lending rate was hoisted to an unprecedented 17 per cent, throwing the plan for an interest-free loan out the window. The only solution was to revise the development downwards, retaining as many of the key proposals as possible. The good news was, that although the estimated cost was cut by half, major improvements could still be included in the plan.

Work began towards the end of 1980 to create a separate dining-room, to improve the bar, and to increase the area of the sun lounge. One welcome improvement was lowering the main windows overlooking the course to enhance the view from the lounge. Members will recall that a decade ago that in order to get a good view of the course they had to crane their necks!

The cost of this revised improvement was some £40,000; an interest free loan of £25,000 was obtained from the Federated Breweries and the balance was borrowed from the bank via over-draft facilities. The chairman, the president (Peter Brown) and members of the Development Committee were commended on the result.

The next phase of major Club re-development was approved at an extra-ordinary general meeting held in May, 1984 when chairman Maurice Beck and his development committee announced the following: the building of new men's, ladies' and juniors' locker rooms; the conversion of the then men's locker room into a games room; the extension of the bar area; space for the Professional's workshop.

Construction work began in February of 1985 in snowy conditions, but all building work was completed by early June, two months ahead of schedule. The new locker room building included a communal caddy car section. This development work was under the supervision of Chris Charge, John Gibson, John Duncan and Alex King, who devoted many hours of leisure time to the project thereby saving the Club several thousands of pounds in fees. The total cost of the development was in the region of £200,000.

By this time the clubhouse had received a very attractive face-lift, an open-plan system presenting a more spacious look, with the extension at the North end of the lounge with a split-level floor an added attraction. The upper level could now be screened off, enabling the new Club restaurant (the old Addicts' Bar) to be extended at will to meet various demands. The sun lounge was further enhanced by the installation of patio doors, which have been a great asset in the lovely warm summers of late.

The Entertainments Committee of the early eighties had been very active in fund-raising, enabling extra facilities to be installed in the Club. They included fitting spot-lights for dancing in the ceiling, two portable stages and a much needed high-quality audio rack system complete with the best loud-speakers that money could buy. As usual, the ladies section made a valuable contribution purchasing a new carpet for the sun lounge. Succeeding chairmen and committees have continued the good work of enhancing the Club's facilities; for example, the extension of the balcony over the dance floor and lounge has been completed.

JOTTINGS FROM THE SEVENTIES AND EIGHTIES

In 1972, Gosforth Urban Council, the landlords increased the rent by £400 per annum, to be reviewed every seven years.

At the 18th hole, play was greatly disrupted by the laying of a new sewer by the local authority; careful restoration work was supervised by the late Frank Townley, then chairman of the Greens Committee.

The 'City G.C.' raised more than £1,000 for the funds of the Variety Club of Great Britain, following a successful tournament staged on the Three Mile Course.

David Moffat, in winning the 'Journal Trophy' at Arcot Hall, set a new course record with a second round total of 66.

Andrew McKinna won the Northumberland County Salver at Gosforth G.C. with a nett 66 off 9 handicap playing in trying weather conditions. His brother, Ian, a low handicap player and winner of numerous competitions at the 'City' began a successful run for the Club in the Newcastle and District League.

Marie McRae, wife of the Professional, Sam McRae, was elected County Ladies Captain for the second year running.

In 1973, Marie led Northumberland to national honours with victory in the English Counties Championship (reported fully in a later chapter).

In the Newcastle and District Golf League, the Club continued to hold its own without ever winning the championship in this decade. Successive Captains commend two 'City' men for their outstanding support of the league team – the late Stan Quine and Bill Foster.

Peter Brown, a well-respected member of the 'City', a good player and fine example of neat concentration at all times was elected to be Club Chairman. Peter, a former captain, contributed sterling work for the benefit of the Club over a period of years.

In the winter of 1973–74, the national fuel crisis hit the 'City'. Shortage of fuel caused the committee to close the club lounge except for special events.

For the first time for several years, the financial situation caused some concern: oil-heating services increased by 40 per cent, rates were increased by £1,000 per annum, and there was a substantial rise in the wages bill. As a member of the committee remarked at the time: 'The reality is that no longer can you pay a skilled green keeper the sum of £25 per week'.

The scenic improvement of the course was reported on by Rod McKenzie, then Chairman of the Greens Committee who advocated the purchase of saplings to plant at strategic locations. One member who has shown a special interest in tree-planting at the 'City' is David Moffat. His efforts over the years have resulted in considerable scenic improvement alongside a number of the holes on the 'City' course.

The decade of the 1980's witnessed many major developments affecting the life of the 'City' Golf Club. They included the universal use of the big ball; a new handicapping system; a new stroke index for the 'City G.C.'; the appointment of the first woman Club Secretary at the 'City', Esme Duncan; and later the amalgamation of the offices of Secretary and Professional.

Those ten years also saw the completion of a major Club re-development scheme; witnessed an outstanding attempt to lift the Newcastle and District League Championship for the second time (pipped at the post); and the emergence of the 'City' Junior Golfing Teams as forces to be reckoned with in county competition and Club competition.

This decade also witnessed the 'City G.C.' golf course maintained in fine condition, and acquiring an enviable reputation from golfers from visiting clubs. After four years of work as greens chairman, Chris Charge handed over the reins to John Gibson in 1985. In 1989 the 'City G.C.' was judged to be in the finest condition of any of the local courses.

During these years, people who had made special contributions to the 'City' Club and the game of golf were appointed Honorary Members of the Club. Among people so honoured were: Esme Duncan for her work as Club Secretary; Frank O'Kane for his environmental contributions to the course; Hilda Broadbent, Past Captain and Past President of the Ladies' Section who attained 50 years membership; and George W. Logan, in recognition of his elevation to the Presidency of the English Golf Union in 1987.

THE YEAR . . . 1984

The chairman, Maurice Beck told members at the A.G.M. that the Club's profit for the year was £3,500, and there was a waiting list for full membership of 60.

The excellent condition of the 'City' course was remarked on by the Northumberland County Executive when the county match against Lancashire took place at the Three Mile Bridge. Further praise was expressed by the Lancashire Executive who said that the quality of the 'City' greens was a good as Formby!

Out of 417 male members, including Juniors, by far the largest number fell into Category 3 players – 190 – so it was hardly surprising that Cat. 3 produced the most competition winners. The most consistent winners were around the 12 handicap mark.

Reporting the various insurance claims made by the Club during the year, the Treasurer reported the sum of £2,800 received following the theft of the 'Chronicle Cup'. This was a tragic loss for the City of Newcastle Club who, winning the Inter-County Foursomes no fewer than seven times had made the trophy their own. The large solid silver trophy, held with pride, was chained to a corner of the Hylton Room as it then was. But the thief entered the premises in broad daylight, quickly cut through the chain and smuggled the cup out under a raincoat. It was a coincidence that the visiting party playing the course that day was a party of Policemen!

THE YEAR . . . 1985

Chairman Brian Goldwater, reporting to the A.G.M. on the fulfilment of the major development project, revealed that the new locker room building provided 448 lockers for men and 102 for ladies. The opening up of the old entrance hall to form an extended bar area had proved popular with members.

The Steward, Mr. Alan Jobson left the Club after only a short stay, and he was succeeded by Mr. Malcolm Angus.

The 'City' course was well presented when it hosted the Northumberland County 72-hole stroke-play competition. During this championship, the course record was broken by Neil Graham of Newcastle United with a score of 67. (The present course record was set in 1989 by Michael Blackburn).

Under the new handicapping system, the trend has been for handicaps to move upwards. Although category 1 players won the scratch competitions, they did not win any handicap competition in 1985.

The Juniors, who only joined the Northumberland Junior League in the late 1970's were starting to make their presence felt in 1985. Under their captain, David Steven they finished in the top half of the league with some very good results.

The Club secretary, Mrs. Esme Duncan was commended at the A.G.M. 'for the smooth, efficient and friendly way she has handled sometimes difficult office affairs'.

THE YEAR . . . 1986

Chairman John Duncan told members at the A.G.M. that the surplus of £836 'was very disappointing and much lower than budgeted for' in the 1985–86 accounts. That was mainly due to the bad weather which meant that the green fees income of some £12,000 fell way short of expectations.

It was found that the new snooker table was not being played as much as expected, vindicating the committee's decision to install only one table despite pressure from some members to install two.

Mr. Duncan reported that members should stand by for a steep increase in course rental (Newcastle Corporation are the owners of the land). The initial assessment was an increase from £1,650 per year to nearly £10,000 per year. John Duncan was confident that this could be reduced (It was).

'The 'City' under Captain W. McAndrew finished in a creditable 5th position in the Newcastle and District Golf League, the highest placing for a considerable time.

The performance of the Ladies' Teams were commended by the Chairman. The first team finished 4th in the first division, a very good performance bearing in mind the strength of competing teams. The Ladies Second Team gave a very creditable performance, coming away with runners-up medals in their division.

When the 'City' appointed Esme Duncan as Club secretary in 1980 the Club was something of a fore-runner in appointing a woman for this post for the first time. When Mrs. Duncan retired from the secretaryship in 1986, the 'City' again blazed something of a trail in golfing administration when they appointed Anthony Matthew, the Professional as the new Secretary, combining duties of both posts.

John Gibson, chairman of the Greens Committee reported after the 'City' hosted the County Fixture against Cheshire, that the Cheshire Captain declared that the condition of the course was 'magnificent'.

Young 'City G.C.' golfers playing in the Northumberland Junior League established themselves as a force and had one of their best seasons ever. Members of the team and alternates for places were: David Shepherd (Captain), Neil Custis, Graham Taylor, David Smith, John Watson, Phillip Warren, David Duncan, Darren Varley, Andrew Moffat, Julian Pearson and Gary Scott.

At the end of the season, the 'City' Juniors finished joint second. Not to be outdone, a 'City' Junior Angela Parr was at this time a rising star in the team of Northumberland girls.

During the year, one lady member of the 'City G.C.' discovered the 'secret' of shooting holes in 1 (play with the wife of the former 'City' Professional!). Isabel Johnstone recorded her first 'Ace' playing with Marie McRae, her husband Jimmy and Charles Stevenson. At a later date and again playing with Marie McRae, Isabel again holed out in 1 at the 14th hole while marking an E.D.S.

One of the 'City's' fine young golfers, Ian Matthewson won the Captain's Tankard as the team player of the year.

Not many of us who enjoy golf on holiday courses can expect to break course records on official terms but it happened to one 'City' player in 1986. When Charles A'Court, then playing off 5 handicap turned up at the Meon Valley Golf and Country Club, near Southampton he was not to know that an 'Open' Medal Competition was in progress. Given permission to enter, Charles returned a 69 minus 5 giving him a nett 64 which set a new course record. His fine round on that course measuring 6,500 yards also included a hole in 1 at the 153 yard 12th hole.

The Club Championship was retained by Aidan Harrison with rounds of 77 and 72, returning 149.

THE YEAR . . . 1987

England defeated Scotland in the annual fixture by 4½ matches to 1½.

Complaints about slow play at busy periods and on competition days led the committee to introduce course stewards with the authority to impose penalties.

'City' character and veteran golfer Gwynne Jones (deceased), who served the 'City G.C.' in various offices over the years, including Club Captain, was elected an honorary member of the Senior Golf League Executive, as well as an honorary member of the 'City' Senior Golf Section (of which he was a founder member).

The Secretary and organiser of the 'City' Section of the Senior League, Bill Elder reported an 'eventual' hole in 1 at the 2nd hole using a 5 iron. Playing in a four-ball with Joe Steele, Chris English and Arthur Brown in freezing fog, no one saw where the ball finished. An extensive search and rake around the back of the 2nd discovered nothing. Joe Steele said, 'Perhaps its in the hole'. It was, to give Bill his first 'Ace' in 26 years of golf.

David Moffat, who first won the Club Championship in 1954 won the Championship in 1987 for the eighth time. He shot 73 plus 76 = 149.

After studying a total of more than 1,200 players' cards from 11 competitions at the 'City', the committee drew up a new stroke index, in preparation for the 1988 season.

As from April 1st, 1988 the committee decided that all Club competitions, including Stableford and Bogey would be played from the medal tees. The only exceptions would be certain drawn competitions which could still be played from the boxes.

Mike Wilkes and Bob Blackett won the County Members Spring Meeting.

Ros Hunter won the Ladies' Club Championship.

A new Past Captain's Trophy, for competition on Stableford terms was presented by John Sleight (Captain, 1977). 'City' golf captains turned out in force to see Jim Slater come home the winner after a 3-way tie (Jim Browning and Eric Mason lost it on the back 9).

The annual general meeting approved an increase in subscriptions by £10 to £170. There were still many more applicants to join the 'City' than the Club could take.

After the Club Treasurer (Mr. John Duncan) reported that after the Club had been notified of an increase in annual rent to nearly £10,000, negotiations were entered into. After successful representation he was able to report that the new figure had been reduced to £6,700. At the A.G.M. the Treasurer and the Committee were both congratulated on the favourable outcome of the rent review.

Teams from the Ladies' Section were congratulated on performing creditably in the 1st and 4th Divisions of the County Leagues.

On the course, the great 'City' 'Battle of the Bunkers' continued. In this regard the Greens Committee threw in new 'reserves' and Chairman John Gibson reported that many greenside bunkers had been dug out, rebuilt and refilled with a special range of sand. Work on further improvements was to continue. Complaint was made that some members and their invited guests were reluctant to remove footprints after playing from the sand.

A review of competitions in the year showed that golfers within Categories 2 and 3 Handicaps won the vast majority of trophies and prizes, winning 21 out of 27 qualifying competitions). The highest number of playing members was in Catergory 3 (13 – 20 handicap), totalling some 41% of the whole.

The Greens Chairman complained that 'a high number of members' were not submitting returns of their competition scores'. It was felt they were not making a genuine attempt to complete the course, which was not within the spirit of the new handicapping system.

The A.G.M. agreed that from April, 1988 Junior members would be allowed to play in Men's Competitions and to win both trophies and vouchers.

The Club had a total of 463 playing members in 1987. During the 1986–87 season there were more than 5,590 competitors in both winter and summer competitions.

THE YEAR . . . 1988

Norman Finkle and Jim Slater won the County members Autumn meeting at Whitley Bay with a nett 68.

At the A.G.M., Chairman Alex King reported that the 'City' League Team finished joint second in the second division Team Championship and gained promotion to the first division. He also reported that the Ladies Team had finished in fourth position in the first division and third in the fourth.

As a result of the Variety Club of Great Britain tournament staged at the 'City', some £28,000 was raised for charity – enough to buy three 'Sunshine Coaches'.

Chairman of Greens, John Gibson, reported a considerable improvement in the condition of the fairways, due to the purchase of a new set of hydraulic gang-mowers.

In the 1988 season some 61% of the winners of qualifying competitions were from Category 3 Handicap (13 – 20).

The introduction of the variable standard scratch score more accurately reflected the playing conditions on the day, and as a result slowed down the upward movement of handicaps.

There was a tremendous tussle for top spot in the Club Championship between Aidan Harrison and Michael Blackburn. Level after 36 holes, they were still joint leaders after 54 holes. After a three hole play-off, Michael nudged ahead to win by one shot.

There was also a tight finish in the final of the Collings Trophies when two father and son combinations met head on. All square after 18 holes, David and Andrew Moffat beat Eric and David Steven on the 19th.

The annual England v Scotland match was cancelled as a result of lack of support from the Club's Scottish contingent.

Darren Varley won the Junior Club Championship with a score of 73 (gross).

THE YEAR . . . 1989

At the Annual General Meeting, John Gibson, chairman of Greens reported a season played on a course in very good condition, with hard-running fairways and receptive but true greens. The major problem centred on the tees, where lack of artificial watering and heavy traffic had caused extensive wear.

The number of full-time greens staff had been increased from four to five.

One unfortunate occurrence during the year was the removal from the clubhouse of the Competitions Book – not only causing much extra work in checking through all competitions for the year, but making any analysis of the results impossible.

Mr. Gibson announced important changes in the Handicap System which included the following: scores returned by category 3 and 4 players in qualifying competitions away from home no longer qualify for handicap increases; under rule 19, handicap increases could be awarded to category 3 and 4 players by their Handicap Sub-Committee.

Members playing in category 3 won the lion's share of the season's competitions, 17 out of 28, or some 60%. The next highest category of winners was category 4 with 7 winners or 25%.

The Treasurer, Mr. P. W. A. Brown reported an increase of revenue over the previous year of some £18,000, due mainly to bar profit, pin machines and green fees showing increases. (That figure excluded income from subscriptions.) A surplus of £3,912, was reported, gratifying after meeting costs from the first year of the five-year machinery replacement plan.

Two former 'City G.C.' Captains – Arthur Smith and John Sleight – set up a new County Captain's record in winning the Society of Northumberland Golf Captains Autumn meeting with a score of 50 points (Stableford).

INTO THE NINETIES

Michael Blackburn, who already was course record holder at the 'City G.C.' played a dream round in August when he smashed the course record at Hexham with a 65. Playing in the Dunhill Amateur Masters Regional Qualifier, he went out in 32 and came back in 33 on the challenging Hexham course to return a five under par card.

By winning the Club Championship, Aidan Harrison made it a hat-trick of wins. He was also victorious in 1985 and 1986.

David Shepherd recorded a fine win in the Northumberland Junior Stroke Play Championship, to become the third 'City G.C.' Junior to carry off this honour. He was also the 'City G.C.' Junior Champion for 1989.

The winner of the 1990 'City G.C.' Junior Championship was Andrew Moffat.

The drive-in day by the new Captain, Jack Spencer was an unqualified success, opening the proceedings with a long drive down the middle of the first fairway.

The 'City G.C.' Senior League Teams had their best year to date – they finished 6th in the Northumberland League after gaining top spot for a short time in the summer.

The Northumberland Senior Field Day Winner was the Captain of the 'City', Norman Dodds.

At the annual general meeting in October, the Chairman's Report was presented by Alex King; Brian Goldwater was elected President; Maurice Beck, Vice-Captain; and Chris Miller, Treasurer.

Members were informed at the A.G.M. that an old, respected member and former President, the late Jim Taylor had left £500 in his will for the installation of a new exterior clock for the clubhouse. A plaque to the memory of an eminent President, Sir Stephen Easten (President of the 'City G.C.' 1932–1937) has been added.

John Gibson reported that there were 469 male playing members, of which the largest number fell into Category 3 Handicap (13 – 20). During 1990, there had been some 6,000 entries in competitions held at the 'City G.C.'

In the summer of 1991 Chris Charge was elected Centenary Year Vice-Captain.

Illustrations

Top: The Newcastle and District League Squad for the 1991 playing season.
Pictured from L. to R: B. Simpson, P. Smith, A. Stevenson, D. Shepherd, S. McKenna, D. McCardle, M. Blackburn, J. Spencer (Capt.), A. Harrison, D. Moffat, G. Gill, K. Cairns, G. Williamson, T. Miles, C. A'Court and A. Leigh.

Bottom: The Committee of the City of Newcastle Golf Club 1990/91.
Front, L. to R: Arthur Wraith, Alex King (Chairman), Jack Spencer (Captain) and John Gibson.
Back, L. to R: Maurice Beck (Vice Capt. when picture taken and Centenary Year Capt.), Colin Hewitt, Peter Smith, Chris Miller (Treasurer), Joe Farley, Anthony Matthew (Secretary and Professional), Geoffrey Harrison, Bill Smith and Arthur Smith.

Top: A rare photograph for the following reasons. In 1950 the Northumberland County Championship was played at 'The City', and both the winner and the losing finalist were from the 'City'. Bill Blake, the winner is congratulated by Edgar Gray.

Bottom: Triple county winners in 1946/47 from the City of Newcastle G.C.
Pictured L. to R: Arthur Black, Ernie Sullivan, Edgar Gray and Philip Richardson. Between them, they won the County Championship, the County Club Championship and the Inter-County event known as the 'Chronicle Cup'.

Top: Taking a breather while playing 200 holes! Amazing feats performed on the 'City' course were the great golfing marathons of 1960 and 1961. John Duncan and David Beardall were chasing the World Endurance Record for the highest number of holes played in one day.

Bottom: A quarter of a century after his golfing marathon, John Duncan driving off the first tee at 'The City' in his Captain's year of 1985.

Top: The one and only Stan Quine, a great club character and loyal servant to the end.

Bottom left: Captain's Day, 1977. Taking time out at the turn are Don Lishman (foreground) and John Thompson, a former Club Captain and well-respected Club Chairman.

Bottom right: Harry Pearson, a popular member for many years, is pictured trapped in 'tiger country' during a Captain's Day round.

Norman Finkle (top) and Gwynne Jones, two Past Captains of the Club who gave extended service to 'The City' in various roles, including chairmanship of committees. Finkle was also Club Chairman.

Former Sunderland footballer, Ben Clark, a 'City' member for many years, created a niche for himself in local golfing history by winning the County Salver in 1990. By so doing, he became the only Northumberland golfer to have won both the Salver and the Foster Cup.

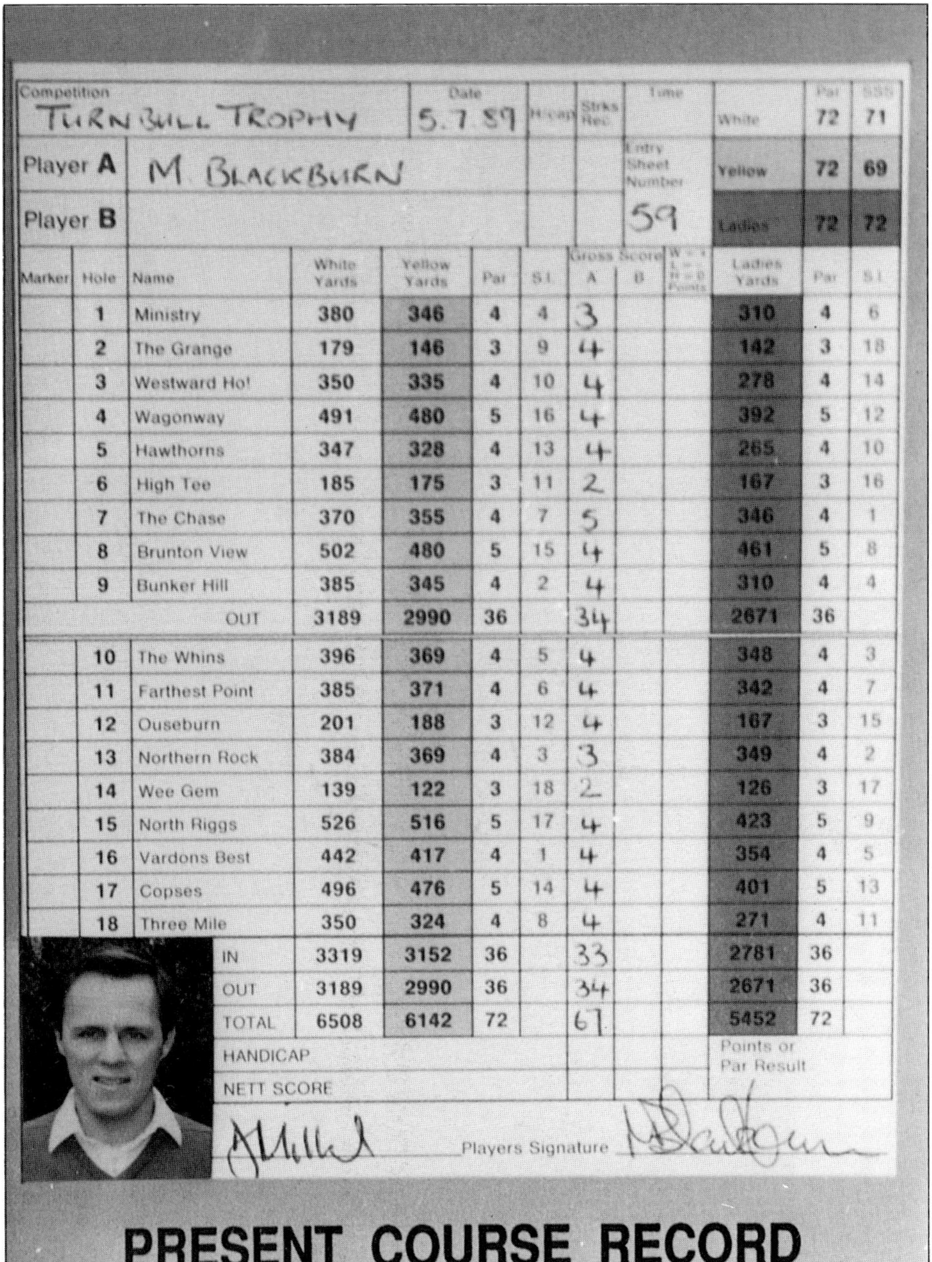

Competition	Date	H'cap	Strks Rec	Time		Par	SSS
TURNBULL TROPHY	5.7.89				White	72	71
Player A: M BLACKBURN				Entry Sheet Number	Yellow	72	69
Player B				59	Ladies	72	72

Marker	Hole	Name	White Yards	Yellow Yards	Par	S.I.	Gross Score A	Gross Score B	W = + L = - H = 0 Points	Ladies Yards	Par	S.I.
	1	Ministry	380	346	4	4	3			310	4	6
	2	The Grange	179	146	3	9	4			142	3	18
	3	Westward Ho!	350	335	4	10	4			278	4	14
	4	Wagonway	491	480	5	16	4			392	5	12
	5	Hawthorns	347	328	4	13	4			265	4	10
	6	High Tee	185	175	3	11	2			167	3	16
	7	The Chase	370	355	4	7	5			346	4	1
	8	Brunton View	502	480	5	15	4			461	5	8
	9	Bunker Hill	385	345	4	2	4			310	4	4
		OUT	3189	2990	36		34			2671	36	
	10	The Whins	396	369	4	5	4			348	4	3
	11	Farthest Point	385	371	4	6	4			342	4	7
	12	Ouseburn	201	188	3	12	4			167	3	15
	13	Northern Rock	384	369	4	3	3			349	4	2
	14	Wee Gem	139	122	3	18	2			126	3	17
	15	North Riggs	526	516	5	17	4			423	5	9
	16	Vardons Best	442	417	4	1	4			354	4	5
	17	Copses	496	476	5	14	4			401	5	13
	18	Three Mile	350	324	4	8	4			271	4	11
		IN	3319	3152	36		33			2781	36	
		OUT	3189	2990	36		34			2671	36	
		TOTAL	6508	6142	72		67			5452	72	
		HANDICAP								Points or Par Result		
		NETT SCORE										

Players Signature

PRESENT COURSE RECORD

Michael Blackburn set a new course record of 67 while competing in the Turnbull Trophy in July, 1989. Out in 34 and back in 33, his record score included eight birdies. He followed that up by smashing the course record at Hexham in August, 1990 with a 65.

Trophy Night 1990.

Top left: John Gibson, winner of the Calcutta Cup.

Top right: Dave McCardle who carried off the Pendower Medal.

Bottom: Aidan Harrison receives the Club Championship Trophy from Norman Dodds, the 1990 Captain.

Top left: Stephen Lamb, winner of the Pease Coronation Cup.

Top right: David Moffat, who won the Pease Medal.

Bottom: Past Captain Norman Dodds wishes the newly-elected Captain, Jack Spencer good luck during his year of office.

Ernie Sullivan, an outstanding player who won countless honours on the golf course. He played off scratch, or better, for many years at 'The City'. He carried only seven or eight clubs though his shrewd golfing brain enabled him to play good golf to the day he died.

Chapter XI

SOME OUTSTANDING 'CITY' PLAYERS

The Golfing Magic of Ernie Sullivan

The outstanding feat and golfing accomplishment of Ernie Sullivan was that he played off scratch or better for more than 40 years at the 'City'. His name appears on the Club Honours' Boards more than 30 times; he won the Pease Medal and the Pendower Medal no fewer than seven times. When he was three score years and ten, Sullivan was still striking the ball well which – accompanied by his guile and golfing shrewdness – allowed him to win an occasional competition even then. Born in 1884 in Northumberland, he played on both the Moor and the Three Mile Bridge courses.

He also played for the Northumberland County team. Though he earned a title different from all the rest: 'The best Northumberland golfer never to win the county championship.' He was favourite to win on more than one occasion, but so unpredictable and tantalizing is the golf game that he was never destined to win. In one particular year he was the strong favourite to carry off the county title after defeating the holder, Ralph Thompson in a great battle in the last eight.

In the final, the fates were against him and he was beaten by a four-handicap man, Errington Dunford. At the time, Sullivan was playing off plus two.

Ernie Sullivan had spent his formative years in that little pearl of Northumberland golf – Alnmouth Village. He soon caught the 'bug' which was never to leave him until the day he died. When he moved South to work in Newcastle he joined the Town Moor Club for a time. But he soon moved onto the 'City' where his talents attained their peak, settling down to a long period of outstanding good golf.

The Sullivan success story would surprise the modern day golfer, who usually prefers a largish bag bulging with woods or metals, irons and the wedge making up the official limit of 14 clubs. Ernie always played with a short set of clubs, never more than seven or eight. He would not have the wedge at any price. 'A dangerous and stupid club' he once called it. He used to say, 'Why use a wedge when a canny chip shot would do just as well'. But he did not mind the 'Texas Wedge' – he could use the putter from off the green with deadly results.

Sullivan's golfing strategy was built on the principle of the fewer irons in the bag, the more constant use and feel, creating great confidence in every club and almost total control. Colleagues like the late Gwynne Jones who played with him said that Ernie had the ability to manufacture golf shots at will.

Sullivan once said to his old and faithful partner, Gilly Boswell, 'These new-fangled players carry so many clubs they don't know what to do with them. If they had the numbers off, they would'nt know which club to take!' If Ernie was playing with a stranger he used to tell him, 'Take no notice of the club I take'.

No one played the par 3's at the 'City' quite like him, though he was always on the green for one. For example on the short 14th. he would run the ball on with a longish iron. According to Gwynne Jones, 'Ernie was the straightest hitter in the club – you never had to look for a ball when you played with him. He did not carry many clubs – but the ones he had he could make them talk'.

Sullivan' who was not the wealthiest man in the 'City' and used to arrive at the Club on his motor-cycle was, after some years asked to be a captain. His reply was, 'If it doesn't cost me more than £5, I'll be pleased to do it'. He was duly elected and saved his hard-earned five pounds to buy the prizes on Captain's Day.

If Ernie, never won the county title, he won many a match with his life-long friend, Gilly Boswell. As partners they were rarely beaten. To be confronted by the Sullivan-Boswell partnership in competition was a daunting prospect for opponents. Seemingly the two men were still playing as well as ever when they reached their seventies. Sullivan was supreme in Foursomes and Matchplay; his other favourite partner, Edgar Gray, was an outstanding golfer in his own right. Together they won the 'Newcastle Chronicle Cup' three times in five years. One of Ernie's favourite tournaments was the Northumberland County Clubs' Championship. He was a member of the winning team on at least five occasions: the last time, in 1946, when he was more than 60 years old.

His game was so solid he could not stop winning despite his age.

In the annual 'City' Greensome competition in 1958, Sullivan, then aged 74 and partnered by Boswell (also over 70) came out winners after giving strokes to the losing finalists.

The partnership was only broken by Ernie Sullivan's death the following year, in 1959 – he passed away playing his favourite game on the course that he loved, the 'City'. And a few weeks before he died, he went round the 'City' course in his age – 75.

GILLY BOSWELL
The Romany Scratch Golfer

Gilly Boswell matched his life-long friend, Ernie Sullivan for prowess on the golf course and played off scratch or better for 37 years. Gilly was the more colourful character, making a featish of always turning out to play the game in immaculate dress. Contemporaries recall that more often than not, plus fours were relieved by a fashion pull-over with white shoes and cap to match. His swing matched his elegance on the course, slow, methodical and always graceful.

Boswell was different from any other Club member in that he was a Romany, which perhaps explained that when he was on song, he could make his clubs play a tune . . . .

Gilly joined the 'City' from the old Benton Park club after the second World War. He was twice Club Champion at the 'City', won numerous other trophies and represented his county.

He loved to have Sullivan as his partner. A 'City' member who often saw them in action recalls their expertise in working the ball, starting with the tee shot. While Sullivan hit his tee shots with a pronounced fade, Boswell drove off in the manner of the great Bobby Locke, swinging the ball far out right to return every time to the fairway. Both players were masters of the half-shot, carried a limited number of clubs, each of which they could work with the artistry of a maestro.

Perhaps rather surprisingly, Boswell never won the County Championship nor did he ever reach the final. In other county events, with partners, he was always a force and triumphed on more than one occasion. In 1939, with David Moffat's father he carried off the Northumberland and Durham Inter-County Foursomes Title. In later years the great character called Gilly Boswell left Tyneside to settle in Spalding, Lincolnshire.

THE EDGAR GRAY STORY
The 'City's' 'Mr. Consistency'
Four Times County Champion

One of the finest golfers to play at the 'City' of Newcastle G.C. was Edgar Gray – who played scratch or very low handicap golf for more than 30 years – and who won many honours at County level. He won the Northumberland County Championship four times, between 1927 and 1946, and was runner-up on at least one other occasion.

He was held in high esteem by David Moffat, who, as a young man was often his partner in the late 1950's and early sixties, presenting a formidable combination. After winning the strongly contested Northumberland–Durham Inter-County foursomes in 1956, Moffat told the Press: 'Edgar and I are always happy playing together, even when we aren't playing too well, that's why we won'.

Gray, who joined the 'City' more than 60 years ago was a mathematics teacher who applied deep, analytical thinking to the game of golf. Although he was not a slow player, everything was well thought out. 'He was an outstanding golfer and a wonderful iron player' said Moffat, 'As well as being a long hitter he had a very good short game. Confronted by a difficult shot, he would take his time then give it everything. He was a positive thinker, was never beaten in his own mind and could win from any position'.

Becoming a junior member of the 'City' in the 1920's, Gray was chosen as a boy international in 1926. From then on his golfing career went from strength to strength. At Club level he accumulated countless trophies over the years: one of his most prodigious feats was to win the Pease Medal off scratch no fewer than 12 times, the first time in 1927 and the last in 1961, a span of 34 years.

This former Club champion was a great force in county competition over a long period. His Northumberland Championship wins were in 1927, 1934, 1939; and after serving in the Royal Air Force in World War II, came back to win the championship again in 1946. With different partners over an extended period, Gray had much success in the 'Chronicle Cup' (The Northumberland-Durham Inter-County Foursomes). His first victory was in 1929 playing with Ernie Sullivan and his last in the 1950's playing with David Moffat.

The City of Newcastle G.C. was a dominant force in county golf in the post-war years, prominently led by Edgar Gray. He was a member of 'City' Teams that twice held Northumberland and Durham County Trophies concurrently, as well as the Northumberland Teams Championship.

The 'City' Squad that first brought off a hat-trick of county wins was Gray, Arthur Black, Ernie Sullivan and Philip Richardson, taking the 'Chronicle Cup' (1947) the County Club Championship (1946) with R. E. Gray lifting the Championship Title (1946).

The second 'City' Squad to become a force in county golf was Gray, Moffat, George Wilkinson and John Duncan, winning the 'Chronicle Cup' (1959), the County Club Championship (1959) with David Moffat twice winning the County Championship (1958 and 1959).

For many years, Gray was a member of the 'City' League team taking the younger members of the team in the 1950's (like John Duncan and David Moffat) under his wing, passing on the wrinkles of competing in tough league matches.

Looking back on Gray's career, one recalls that he was very young when he became an accomplished golfer – he won his first County Championship at the age of 17, almost certainly the youngest player to win that coveted event.

John Duncan remembers that Gray was a perfectionist. 'He would spend hours and hours on the practice ground and was an outstanding iron player' said John, 'He was one of the few amateurs before the war who could play a 1 iron off the fairway'.

John tells a lovely tale of Gray employing mind over matter during the 1960 qualifying rounds of the County Championship at the Gosforth Club. Drawn early in the morning, Edgar Gray carded two 76's and arriving back at the clubhouse ruled himself out of qualifying with a total of 152. With nothing to lose, he went to the bar taking 'the medicine' for some considerable time. It came as something of a cold douche to be told later that day that he was involved in a qualifying play-off and was required to play another 18 holes! He said to John Duncan, who was with him: 'You'd better caddy John. Watch every ball as I'll need all my concentration to hit the ball!' Despite his intake, Gray emerged the winner of the play-off and returned to play in the Championship on the morrow, a rather sobered fellow . . . .

John summed up Edgar Gray. 'He could be bad-tempered with himself as he was a perfectionist, but I loved to play with him. He was a generous, kind-hearted man'.

Nobody enjoyed his golf more than Edgar, and few people can have had an extended career over so many years played at such a high level.

KEN FISH

The contribution by Ken Fish to Club, league and county golf can only be described as a major one. Joining the 'City' more than 40 years ago he has been committee man, club President, and when he was elected Club Captain in 1964 he was the youngest Captain ever. Now, in 1991, he is the senior surviving Captain of the Club.

Ken Fish won the Club Championship as far back as 1952 when the 'City' was a force in county golf. One Newcastle golf correspondent, reporting the 'City' Presentation of Trophies for that year, spoke in glowing terms of the 'City' achievements. 'I doubt if any club has staged such an imposing list of prize-winners as The City of Newcastle. I am certain that no club has made such a contribution to local golf' said the journalist. Other prize-winners that night with Ken Fish included Gillie Boswell and 16 years old David Moffat.

Ken's contribution to county golf was equal to his extensive work for the 'City'. Serving on the Northumberland County Executive for 10 years, he was also chairman of the Northumberland Junior Federation and Secretary of the Northumberland Junior Golfers. In fact he has always shown great enthusiasm for bringing on young golfers at whatever level.

On the local golf league scene, Ken Fish represented the 'City' team for many years, eventually ending up as Chairman of the Newcastle and District Golf League.

He has been a fine, low handicap golfer all his life and in a head-to-head battle was always hard to beat, the display of considerable fighting qualities being a feature of his game. He was selected to play for the Northumberland County Colts Team as far back as 1951.

Ken was also responsible in 1967 for establishing close links with Whitley Bay G.C.' represented by Derek Rosenvinge, a liaison that has resulted in the playing of an annual Captain's Match. Ken's innovative qualities for the game showed itself in the nineteen seventies when, again with Derek Rosenvinge, he came up with the idea of forming a Society of Northumberland Golf Captains. The success of the latter has been quite outstanding. Apart from organising golfing events for members, it has brought together former Captains and old friends from all corners of Northumberland at events like the annual dinner and prize-giving. For the record there was a total of 225 past-captains at the 1990 event!

JOHN F. DUNCAN

The Club Champion with a record score, Northumberland County player, member of the City of Newcastle team that won the League Championship and an active member for some 40 years.

That is the record of John F. Duncan, who has also made a great contribution towards the running and administration of the Club, not least as Club Treasurer for 14 years.

Tracing John Duncan's golfing history, one notes that he was only 10 years old when he first swung a club as a junior member of Ponteland G.C. In 1952 when he was 15, he joined the 'City G.C.' with a handicap of 4 and was selected for the County Colts (the equivalent of the County Second Team) the following year.

Following national service in the Army, he returned to civilian life becoming one of the finest players at the 'City' by the late 1950's. In 1959, off 2 handicap, he won the Club Championship with scores of 69 and 71 – a record score of 140 which still stands. (That day he beat David Moffat by six shots, David being the runner-up with a score off 146.)

Competing in the Club Championship the following year, John tied for first place with Edgar Gray and George Wilkinson, losing the play-off to Mr. Gray.

Other low handicap men playing at the 'City' in this period included Arthur Black, Geoff Gill and Fred Cowley. In the post-war years, the 'City' presented a golfing force, winning the County Club Championship four times between 1946 and 1958. (In 1958 David Moffat won the first of his five Northumberland Titles.)

John Duncan was a member of a 'City G.C.' squad that set up an unbeaten record – holding three major trophies at the same time on two different occasions – the County Championship, the Inter-County Foursomes and the Team Championship.

If John had to admit to one person helping him in golf more than any other, it would be Edgar Gray, who became something of a golfing institution at the 'City'.

John's fondest memories of him are of the hardened competitor looking after him as a young player in the League, taking him to away matches in his two-seater sports car with two sets of golf clubs and all the gear squeezed into the tiny boot behind them. John played for the 'City' league team for more than 20 years, was a member of the team that lifted the League Championship in 1966.

He also represented Northumberland County for three years, and on six occasions reached the last 16 of the County Championship play-off. Thirty years ago, with David Beardall, John made a bid for the world endurance record for the number of golf holes played in one day, and the drama of this record attempt is captured in later pages.

In 1958, John Duncan won the then County Handicap Trophy with a 72 less 2 giving him a score of 70.

John can recall the excitement of winning the League Championship for the first time. In order to be certain of outright victory, 'The City' had to beat Westerhope 12–0 in the last match. The tension in the clubhouse mounted as 'City' won 11–1 and the result of their nearest rivals, Gosforth was awaited. As it happened on that final day, Gosforth dropped 2 points resulting in victory for The City of Newcastle G.C.

In a non-competitive match during the early 1960's, John recorded on the old course his lowest-ever gross score of 64. Playing with Peter Greenwell, Martin Quine and David Beardall, his score over the 18 holes included 10 birdies.

Apart from his long spell as Club Treasurer, John held various other administrative posts including Club Chairman (1986–87) and House Chairman (1980–83). He was elected Captain of the Club in 1985.

The Duncan family have been something of a force in 'City' golf and still are, with Esme Duncan and their three sons, Gary, Ian and David active and competitive members. John's late father Percy Duncan also gave yeoman service to the Club.

The Club is in debt to John Duncan who, over the years has played a key role in watching over the Club's finances. Examples which come to mind include his involvement in the £200,000 plus clubhouse redevelopment scheme; his efforts to remove the over-draft; and later his successful negotiations with the course landlords resulting in a sizeable reduction of the new rental.

Throughout a long golfing career, he has always been a keen competitor. As recently as 1989 – some 30 years after first winning the Club Championship – John Duncan finished runner-up in that prestigious event.

GEORGE WILKINSON

One of the outstanding characters of the City of Newcastle G.C. is George (Geordie) Wilkinson, former Northumberland pitman, local Councillor, and caddie who became a very good golfer in his own right.

Top: The season is 1958/59 and three coveted county trophies again fall to the 'City G.C.'
L. to R: John Duncan, David Moffat, Tommy Meikle (Capt.), Edgar Gray and George Wilkinson.

Bottom: An historic picture of a Northumberland County Team which was the first county squad to reach the English Counties Final at Burnham and Berrow in the 1950's. Surrey emerged winners. Included in the Northumberland team are a youthful David Moffat and a more mature George Wilkinson (both 'City' players).

Later in his career he made a local name for himself in golf-course maintenance and design.

Although 'Geordie' was always outspoken – and fearless of authority if he thought his cause was right – he was, and is, good company both on and off the course with his rich, local vernacular stamping him out of the ordinary run of members.

Hailing from Coxlodge and working as a miner at Hazelrigg Colliery, George first scented the aroma of the fairways and the magic of the flying white ball when he came to the 'City' to caddy, a means of augmenting his weekly pit wage. At the end of play, the caddies were permitted to play a few holes and this is when George got the bug. Unable to afford the high price for a new set of clubs, George possessed two clubs given to him by his sister-in-law – they were a brassie (2 wood) and a 5 iron, both crafted by a former 'City' professional, James Fryer, (an excellent club-maker who remained with the 'City' for 17 years until leaving in the late 1940's.)

Unable to afford golf balls, George applied himself to practice hitting champagne corks with the two clubs until he fashioned a golf swing. Then he joined the Newcastle United Club in 1946, his aptitude for the game soon bringing him down to single figures. 'One thing I learned playing on the Town Moor was how to manufacture shots into the wind, a technique that has always been useful in competition' said George.

In fact that golfing technique to his bow enabled him to win his first competition at 'The City' – which he joined in 1956 – in very speedy fashion. Accepted as a member on the Tuesday, George played his first medal on the Saturday with Ernie Sullivan as his partner who was off scratch. Unperturbed by the very windy conditions, George returned a score of 72 nett (off 2 handicap) which was good enough to give him his first trophy.

By this time he had become a member of the Northumberland County Squad and one his proudest moments in nearly 50 years of golf was playing for the county in the English Counties Final of 1957. This was a fierce struggle for supremacy against Surrey and there was nothing in the teams: after finishing all square, Northumberland just lost out in the play-off holes on the Burnham & Berrow course. Of all the trophies standing on side-boards in the sitting room of his home, the finalist's silver medal, presented by the English Golf Union, means the most to him. 'I treasure this English Counties Medal more than anything that I won in golf' he said.

Later, George had a good run in the Engish Amateur Championship held at Ganton, near Scarborough, when he knocked out four opponents until being beaten himself. His best performance in national championships followed the following year at Hoylake when, against all the odds he accounted for three Walker Cup players to reach the quarter-finals of the championship.

George never won the Northumberland County Championship, though he was twice a semi-finalist and one year at Ponteland was playing so well, he was confident of reaching the final. Only an electrifying burst of brilliant golf – five 3's in seven holes from the 10th – by Alan Thirlwell stopped him.

For years, George played for the 'City' in the Newcastle and District League and in one extended run was unbeaten at the 'City' in more than four years of matches.

At club level he won many trophies, including the Club Championship four times. The Club Championship he remembers with mixed feelings is the one he won by 1 shot after a return of 144 for 36 holes – he received a letter from the club secretary warning him about slow play when it was his two partners – not him – who were missing the fairway!

Another memory is from 1966 when the 'City' won the League Championship for the first time. 'I was off last that day and knew that I had to win in order to make sure of the championship.' In the event I finished two up and we were home and dry. I'll never forget the big crowd and the buzz surrounding the final green as we came to it' said George.

To give you some idea of the consistency of play of Geordie Wilkinson, he won the Tom Percy Prize for the best average score one season with 71 over 13 rounds in competition.

'Geordie' knows a thing or two about golf and through the years members have gone to him for advice. The number of times I have heard him tell the high handicapper 'to stay doon and tuck in that right elbow'.

Throughout his golfing life he has always included the same two clubs in his bag: the heavy sand wedge which he christened 'the basher' which somehow he could use to play a delicate pitch to the heart of the green, as well fly a ball from a bunker; and his hickory-shafted putter. That putter is more than 200 years old, came from a Scottish craftsman and enabled George to become one of the finest putters in the area, even when striking it off the sweet spot! This off-set, blade 'weapon' was the gift of one Ralph Thompson, an outstanding Northumberland golfer of his day, who once won two local 'Opens' on the same day (At Newcastle United and Gosforth Golf Clubs.)

George thinks that the standard in amateur golf has risen in the last 20 years; with improved teaching methods becoming available for all but particularly for the young golfer, helped by modern aids such as the video camera play-back facility. If he had to name one man who was most responsible for higher standards he would say John Jacobs.

When the John Jacobs driving ranges sprung up in different parts of the country some years ago, followed by the building of new golf courses, George Wilkinson played an important role in the development in the Gosforth Park. His course lay-out for the Wideopen G.C. as it was then called was chosen by Larry Lucas and John Jacobs in preference to others. George supervised the building of the course and became Head Greenkeeper of the new club, now under the new name of 'Parklands'. Also at the 'City' course over the years he assisted the greens staff.

'Geordie' now over 70 and 'not too good on his pins' is no longer able to play the game. 'But I have many happy memories to fall back on, and have built up a sizeable library of golf videos' he said. The former miner – who did not hit his first golf ball until he was 31 – can walk down memory lane with a glow of pride.

His achievements in the game were not small and in some respects he was a very considerable applied thinker of the game of golf; for example, long before it was common practice among top amateurs, he recorded distances from key points on every hole.

'On every new course I played on in championships I made a point of walking the course the day before and recording my distances' he said, before he cracked another joke and bade the author farewell.

DAVID BEARDALL

David Beardall, who in one way or another has been associated with the City of Newcastle G.C. for more than 40 years has a record of service to the game of golf second to none. Apart from his contributions at club level – at both the 'City' and Backworth – perhaps his greatest contribution has been on the Northumberland County scene. His work for County junior golf and as a member of the County Executive is legendary.

David was only 12 years of age when he joined the 'City' as a junior in 1950; he made solid progress with his game and before the age of 20 was playing off single figures. He was a competition winner and in 1958 took both the Turnbull Trophy and the coveted Calcutta Cup. In the early 1960's after some disagreement with the Handicap Committee of the day, he left the 'City' for Backworth G.C. Though he did not sever his connection entirely, retaining social membership over the years.

It was after leaving the 'City' that David became an enthusiastic worker for the Scout Movement, and later for the Association of Boys' Clubs, which pushed his golf into the background. In due course, he returned to the links and in 1977 began his extensive association with County golf.

In that year, he was elected to the Northumberland Union of Golf Clubs, proving an indefatigable member with 14 years service to date. His contribution to the game was recognised in 1985–86 when he was elected President of the County Union, one of the youngest ever Presidents.

Over a long period, David has become well-known for his great help in encouraging young golfers, and in this respect he formed a close association with David Curry, for whom he often caddied in tournaments. Strange as it may seem, it was this connection with the fine young golfer during the year of his County Presidency that caused one of the biggest controversies of his golfing career. He had watched David Curry emerge from the junior pack in the late seventies to become a boy international in 1980. Throughout that decade, Beardall cemented this association and when Curry reached the finals of the Amateur Championship in 1986, David Beardall saw nothing wrong in continuing as his caddy. Because he was County President at the time, and in effect was affiliated in office to the E.G.U., the golfing establishment frowned on the idea.

David was reluctant to break the partnership with Curry, especially during the closing stages of the Amateur Championship, so resisted efforts to stop him. He even sought a ruling from the 'Royal and Ancient' on the rights of a competitor to nominate his own caddie, and the definition of the roles of both Professional and Amateur caddies.

Fortunately for all, there was a happy ending. Beardall was permitted to caddy, and as we all know David Curry became the new British Amateur Champion.

During his career at the 'City' David Beardall also raised eye-brows in some quarters of County golf when the traditionally conservative outlook of the day did not enthuse over two marathon attempts to break the world endurance record. (An account follows in this book.)

Chapter XII

THE 'CITY'S' GREAT GOLFING MARATHON

50 Miles of Non-stop Golf

Round-and-Round for 20 Hours

Probably the most outstanding feats ever witnessed on the course of the City of Newcastle G.C. were two amazing marathon attempts to capture the World Endurance Record for the highest number of holes played in one day.

On both occasions, in 1960 and 1961, the challengers were John Duncan and David Beardall. The world record at the time was 12 rounds of continuous golf – 216 holes – held by two Americans. In the first bid, and with no training or real preparation, John and David managed only 10 rounds in the single day!

Undaunted, they launched another assault on the record the next year with greater preparation and the planning finely tuned. The story that follows is an incredible one, proving several points, not least the theory that speedy play can produce excellent results.

It was at 2.45 on the morning of June 19th, 1961 that Duncan and Beardall stepped onto the first tee at the 'City' to attempt what no other British pair had achieved before. Although the day was fine there was a strong wind blowing, which wasn't going to help, especially as they were to carry their own clubs throughout.

Duncan was described in the local Press as 'a 24-year-old council officer of Glenfield Road, Gosforth', and Beardall as, 'aged 22, a salesman of Polwarth Place, Gosforth'.

Their objective: to complete 12 rounds and one hole before midnight (217 holes). After studying the cards for the day, it was astonishing to discover that between 2.45 a.m. and 11 a.m. the pair had completed no fewer than five rounds of golf. After taking a 40-minute break for breakfast, the pair set out once more and by 7 p.m. had completed another four rounds, making nine in all.

The worst moment of the day for John Duncan was after the evening break of 20 minutes and after 16 hours of continuous golf – weary and foot-sore he faced the challenge of rising again to walk to the first tee and hit yet another drive. His partner's problem was rather more physical, David having required first-aid treatment to bleeding feet. But at 7.30 p.m. the pair walked out to begin the tenth round of the day, on the last stages of their world championship bid.

The fact that the 'City' men were still in fairly good shape was due to some extent by the back-up services on the course, provided by family and friends. At 5.30 a.m. that day Esme Duncan had risen and taken sandwiches out to the two golfers; and in the closing stages at night crates of refreshments were placed on each tee box to rejuvenate the men over the last few rounds.

David Beardall recalls that the most amusing moment of the day took place at the beginning of the ninth round at exactly 5.30 p.m. Watching them play the old 2nd green and staring at them in amazement was a Newcastle Corporation bus driver (on the old course, the second green was tucked into the left hand corner of the present playing field bordering Broadway West). Resting his arms on the stone wall overlooking the green, the bus driver shouted across: 'Aren't you the silly - - - - - - - I saw playing at six o'clock this morning?' David replied: 'We are – but if you read your "Evening Chronicle" you'll see we're going for a golfing world record, and we're not finished yet by a long chalk!' As David said, the bus driver had seen them first thing when he looked out from his trolley-bus waiting at a terminus point.

The 'City' Challengers began their 11th round at 9 p.m. and by the time they had completed 18 holes the light had almost gone. However, they pushed on and completed another two holes to finally register the massive total of 200 golf holes played in well under 24 hours. And while that did not break the world endurance record, it almost certainly registered a new British record for pairs.

This marathon event captured the attention of Press, Radio and Television alike as well as riveting the attention on 'The City' of many Tyneside golfers. The presence of a big Media contingent, plus the teasing, unrelenting wind which added at least 10 minutes to each round, probably cost Duncan and Beardall the world record.

The completion of 200 holes within the same day, covering a distance of some 50 miles is a remarkable physical feat; after all, the majority of us have had enough after playing a 36-hole event.

What perhaps is more praiseworthy is the impressive golf performances by both players throughout the day and the night. Apart from the last round, Duncan returned figures of 73–80 gross for every round; while David Beardall's scores were between 80 and 90 gross throughout the marathon. And what is equally impressive is that Duncan (handicap 3) and Beardall (handicap 6) averaged some 1 hour 40 minutes per 18 holes.

On completion of 200 holes and as darkness fell, Duncan admitted defeat. 'We could have gone on but we would not have finished before midnight' he said. Some 'City' members – caught up in the enthusiasm of the occasion – offered to light up the 'City' fairways with car headlights. But it would have been to no avail.

At the end of it all, both players looked in reasonably good condition though both were very foot-sore. Before the end, Beardall had had one hand bandaged as a protection against blisters. But their spirits were unabashed.

There is nothing so surprising as the game of golf. One would have thought that the day after the golfing marathon the last thought in the mind of John Duncan would have been to go out to play golf. That is exactly what he did! With partner Ken Fish, John Duncan set out to play a Collings knock-out match. When John's partner heard about the marathon, he was less than pleased! As it happened both John and Ken were on their game. . . and came away easy winners.

Chapter XIII
SOME CLUB CHARACTERS . . . .
Unforgettable 'City' Men

THE BOYDS

The late John Henry Boyd and his son, John, currently the longest-serving member of the City of Newcastle G.C., have together been connected with the Club for more than 100 years. Both father and son played key roles in the life of the Club for many years, serving as Honorary Solicitors, one following the other.

John Boyd Senior was a founder member of the new 'City' Club at the Three Mile Bridge and later, in 1924 he joined his son, John who recalls paying a total of five guineas to become a full playing-member.

J. Boyd Senior was elected Captain of the Club in 1932/33. In February of 1933 he made a presentation to the Club of what has become one of our most treasured artefacts – a framed facsimile copy of the original petition to the Freemen of Newcastle to form the Club in June, 1891. Golf apart, he was a keen aviator and was one of the early members of Newcastle upon Tyne Aero Club.

John Boyd, Junior, apart from a short sojourn at Arcot Hall G.C. lasting about a year, has been a playing member at the City for the past 60-odd years. In his early days at the Three Mile Bridge, John recalls that many members wore plus fours and tweed jackets. Although one member, a local lawyer and rather eccentric always played in a frock coat with drain-pipe trousers tucked into long stockings, all the while smoking a fat cigar.

J. Boyd Junior, who in earlier days played off single figures for years established a reputation of being a very quick player. He won the Captain's Day trophy as far back as 1939. His most vivid memory of golf at the 'City' was a round with his father years ago. Playing on the old course, they arrived at the 7th tee box and were waiting to drive. His father was sat contentedly on a nearby seat when a ball whizzed through the air from nowhere, struck him on the chin and knocked him clean out. The striker of the 'pawky' shot was a single figure man suffering a momentary lapse. After a couple of minutes, J. Boyd Senior recovered consciousness to hear apologies all round. With a shake of the head and appropriate comment, he selected his driver, walked onto the tee and hit a good ball down the middle!

GWYNNE JONES

Another member, hailing from Wales originally, contributed sterling service to the club over a period of years. He was the late Gwynne Jones. In an interview before his death in 1989, he related that he, and his wife Eileen joined the 'City G.C.' exactly 40 years ago when there was no entrance fee, and the subscriptions for them both totalled ten guineas.

In a long association with the 'City', both Gwynne and Eileen were elected to the offices of Captain and President of their respective sections. In the years that Gwynne served on committee, he was particularly effective as House Chairman, not only as an organiser of clubhouse events but also as a refurbisher of the club interior.

He played off single figures for many years, had a meticulous approach to the game, swore by his blade putter and in the end always said that the game came down to concentration over the whole 18 holes. He also had a reputation for being one of the best putters in the club in his day, but was known to utter strange words if a member of his four-ball got anywhere near his line when putting. He was always smartly turned out on the golf course, and was a stickler for etiquette.

During his years at the 'City', he partnered some very fine golfers. He often played with Ernie Sullivan, and that other fine low handicap man, Gilly Boswell. He was a strict rules player and extremely difficult to beat in a head-to-head match. Though, for Gwynne, Ernie Sullivan was easily the finest golfer in the Club. 'I had the privilege of playing many games with him' said Gwynne, 'For a long time we enjoyed a four-ball, the late Lennie McNaughton and his brother Fred, both good players, Ernie and myself. If Ernie was rather a dour character, he was none the worse for that, and occasionally he voiced golfing pearls of wisdom which were snapped up and put in the memory bank'.

One of Ernie's sayings was: 'When in match-play with your ball on the green, and you have two putts for a win never try to be clever'. Another: 'When pitching over a greenside bunker always pitch the shot a yard or so past the pin – it's just as easy to putt a yard back to the pin, and the shot allows a greater margin for error'.

Gwynne recalled the life-long friendship between Ernie and Gilly Boswell. As partners on the 'City' course they were a mighty force.

In the latter part of his golfing career, Gwynne Jones was one of the active founders of the Northumberland Senior Members League, of which he was 'City G.C.' secretary and organiser for some years. In recognition of his work for the League he was elected to Honorary Membership.

His widow, Eileen, a past Captain of the Ladies Section and a much respected member of the Club emigrated to Canada on the death of her husband to join her married daughter in Toronto.

SOME OTHER 'CITY' STALWARTS

FRANK HEADS

Frank Heads, who died in 1986 at the age of 83 was a long-serving and respected member of the Club, and a past Captain. He joined the 'City G.C.' in 1944 and remained a member until his death.

A good companion on the course, he was highly entertaining off it. Often in the clubhouse he could be seen regaling colleagues with his dry, witty humour, producting a wealth of stories at will. As Captain of the Club in 1963, he officially opened the re-designed 'City' course.

CHARLES BARTON

The late Charles Barton was an outstanding member and servant of the Club, occupying the post of Club President for no less than six years from 1962. Prior to that he served at Club Captain in 1957 and like other 'City' stalwarts like Tom Percy and Jim Ferris, he served on club committees for many years.

JIM FERRIS

Jim Ferris was a long-serving member, good golfer and greatly respected by club members. He was elected Club Captain for two consecutive years, in 1959 and 1960. In later years, he accepted the post of Club Secretary where he served for several years.

BILL BALFOUR

Bill Balfour, who joined the club in the post-war years gave years of valuable service to club committees. His contribution in various roles led to his election as Club Captain in 1973. As a former Regional Manager for the Goodyear Tyre Company, he became a leading figure in the golfing section of the Motor Traders' Association. Always good company, with a bluff humour and plain speaking, Bill Balfour continues to be a popular 'City G.C.' member.

TOM BRAMWELL AND TOM PERCY

Tom Bramwell and Tom Percy contributed great service to the Club during the late 1950's and the 1960's, not only serving on various Committees but also holding the highest offices of the 'City'.

Tom Bramwell ran a family butchers business in Gosforth, and in addition to giving stalwart service to the Club he was a senior member of the then Gosforth District Council. He served two periods as Chairman of Gosforth Council. In 1961, Mr. Bramwell was elected Captain of 'City' and two years later was made an Honorary Member of the Club in recognition of the services he had rendered over the years. He also served as Club Chairman.

Tom Percy ran a Newcastle Estate Agents business and was able to bring his business knowledge to bear for the advantage of the club over a lengthy period. A long-serving Committee member, he was elected Captain of 'City' in 1962. The last office he occupied in the Club was that of President. He too always had the interests of the Club at heart, and was a tireless worker on behalf of members. It says something, for the manner of his service to the 'City' that after joining in 1945, and first serving the club in the 1950's he did not step down from office until 1972.

PHILIP RICHARDSON

Philip Richardson, who held a senior post at Reyrolles of Hebburn was one of the very good golfers that the 'City' produced after the Second World War. He won a considerable number of trophies over the years including the Pendower Medal (Scratch) on two occasions; the Calcutta Cup and the Pease Coronation Cup. With Edgar Gray, he won the County Club Championship in 1946 and again in 1947. He was also the member of the 'City' Squad that twice held three County Trophies simultaneously in the post-war years.

TOM MEIKLE

Tom Meikle was a stalwart and long-serving member and officer of the Club, joining before the outbreak of World War II. A native of Glasgow, who in his working life was Contracts Manager with Vickers, Newcastle, he is remembered as an outstanding Chairman of the Greens Committee, presenting a well-kept and neatly manicured course.

Mr. Meikle was appointed Club Captain in 1958, later to serve as Club President in 1973, '74 and 75'. Always a competent golfer, even he must have been surprised at the way the Gods smiled on him during a match in 1972, which produced an extended 'purple patch' and the best round of a lengthy golfing career.

In that October match of 1972, he shot nine birdies and a number of pars to return a net score of under 60. The occasion was the Captains versus Presidents match. After that electrifying round Tom said, 'I was hitting the greens in regulation figures and putts were dropping in from all over the green'.

He was partnered by the late Gordon Elliott, this combination delivering a baptism of fire for new Captain Balfour and his playing partner, Brian Bigley.

NORMAN FINKLE

Norman Finkle, who joined the Club in the late 1950's gave long and devoted service to the 'City' during the 1970's. In all he contributed 10 years' service on Committees, serving on the House and then the Greens Committee of which he became Chairman.

Elected Captain of the Club in 1970, he subsequently became Club Chairman and it was in that capacity that he master-minded a major clubhouse re-development scheme which he brought before the members in 1979. As a result of those refurbishments, the clubhouse benefited from a much needed face-lift which also provided more room.

One of the many improvements carried out was to redesign and reposition the lounge windows overlooking the course, making viewing easy and comfortable.

Honours won by Norman Finkle include the Northumberland County Members Competition held at Whitley Bay in 1988 with Jim Slater.

NORMAN DUNCAN

Norman Duncan is the second oldest living member of the 'City', joining the club in the 1930's, and has been a stalwart in the true sense of the word ever since. Although well over 80 years old now, Norman was a very capable golfer in his younger days playing down to 4 handicap. He played off single figures for many years.

During his retirement in the sixties he was asked to accept the position of club secretary. Accepting, he filled the post until the 1970's, a period of 13 years. Prior to that he had served on Club Committees.

He carried out the duties of secretaryship in keen and zealous fashion, always conscious of upholding the long traditions of the Club. One 'City' Captain, for whom Duncan served, said of him: 'Norman could be a bit of a disciplinarian though he was making sure the rules of the Club were followed and achieved. As an officer of the Club he projected a very good image which was often commented on by leading golf officials on their visits to the Three Mile Bridge'. On the course, the behaviour of Norman was impeccable. Always a quick player himself, he could not tolerate players holding up play. A man of firm and honest character, he was never slow to express his views about the etiquette of the game. Norman's playing career extended until 1990 when – in his eighties – he decided to call it a day.

BILL FOSTER

Joining the 'City' more than 30 years ago, when he was over 50 Bill Foster was the living proof that age need not necessarily be a bar to playing good golf. In his hey-day at the 'City' Bill played off 5 handicap, though in his mid-seventies he was still off single figures, winning the Garland Cup for the second time in 1981 at the age of 74.

Any young aspiring golfer would have done well to study the methods of this man; carrying a placid temperament he was never ruffled by the games of opponents, was blessed with a smooth putting stroke which often was enough 'to win him the money'.

Bill played occasionally for the 'City' League Team, and among the trophies he won was The Collings twice (First with the late Ted Magnay as partner and later with Arthur Smith). For many years he played every week with a namesake, the late Syd Forster who died suddenly on the course in 1969.

Before arriving at the 'City', Bill was a prominent member of Consett G.C., playing regularly for their North-West League Team and winning the Club Championship in 1953. After moving to Bishop Auckland in 1947, he also became Club Champion of that club in 1956.

After he retired, Bill Foster could often be seen working away at jobs on the 'City' course. One of his achievements was to improve the passage over the burn, which runs across the 1st and the 18th, laying large wooden sleepers.

His son, Peter Foster, joined the 'City' in 1959 and was soon recognised as a very promising player indeed. Indeed, Professional Sam McRae offered him a job as Assistant Professional in the early 1960's, which he accepted. In time, Peter moved on, gaining experience in the Professional Shops of various other clubs until he settled at Kilton Forest G.C. Workshop, where he was appointed Club Professional, making a great success of it.

JOE STEELE

One of the real characters of the 'City' over a period of many years going back to the 1950's has been Joe Steele. Always good company on the course, with rarely a dull moment he can be at his best when discoursing on the finer points of the Sport of Kings. He is one of the few players in the North of England who can translate the racing vernacular into apt and racy descriptions of match-play golf.

Joe is thought to be 'The Peter Pan' of the 'City', ageing not, retaining a youthful figure and still running for charity. He also is a member of that school who believe that to play quick golf is to play golf well, a technique that has won him not a few honours.

Walking down memory lane, he recalls reaching the final of the Collings Trophies in 1958 when they came up against two veterans, whose combined age was 148 years.

He and his partner, Harry Hindmarsh were on form at this time but had the misfortune to face the outstanding golfing skills of Ernie Sullivan (75 years) and Gillie Boswell (73) who coasted to a 5 and 4 victory.

However, Steele and Hindmarsh made amends the next year by setting a record for the Olivers Trophies on the old course with a score of 9 up, played as a greensome then with handicaps limited to 18. In those days, that was a very good score.

HARRY HINDMARSH

Among the group of golfers who came over to the 'City' after World War II from the old Benton Park Golf Club was Harry Hindmarsh, a fine player who retained his low single figure handicap for many years. He won the City Club Championship three times as well as many other trophies. His contemporaries always said he could have achieved even greater honour had he not suffered an occasional tendency to blow-up in the closing stages of a tournament.

An old colleague, the late Gwynne Jones once said; 'Harry was a fine player, though after playing say 15 holes in par, one set-back at the next hole could finish him'. For a long time he played off 3 handicap, and Joe Steele remembers him as a formidable player indeed. Hindmarsh was twice a member of 'City' teams that won the County Club Championship. In 1954, he and Edgar Gray won the 'Chronicle Cup'.

FRANK TOWNLEY

The late Frank Townley was one of the great workers for the City of Newcastle Golf Club; he gave years of service both on the Greens Committee and as Chairman of the Club. Under his guidance during the early 1970's the course surgery at the 18th, when a new sewer was laid, turned out to be a successful if trying operation. As Greens Chairman he saw the provision of a pop-up sprinkler system and proper housing for the course equipment. And as Club Chairman he supervised the refurbishment of the locker room.

Those who worked with Frank on committee remember him as a dour and doughty fighter who, once embarked on a course of action would thrust it through to a successful conclusion.

Perhaps there was only one area where he had to admit to some defeat, and that was improving the state of the course bunkers. In the 'City Magazine' of 1974 he wrote: 'While the layout of the course is excellent, there could still be improvement – for example the bunkers. Over the years, the Greens Committee have tried out various kinds of sand but every one, in the end has turned out unsatisfactory. You will have noticed we are now trying out a new kind of red sand in the 2nd hole bunkers. But I would like to see the scientists brought in to tackle the problem'.

It is not perhaps surprising that the 'City' Course, open as it is to South Westerlies and Northerlies has always faced the problem of maintaining all bunkers in prime condition.

Frank Townley, who had suffered as a Japanese prisoner-of-war was rarely one hundred per cent fit, and the Club suffered a great loss when he passed away before his time.

ROD MACKENZIE

Like his contemporary, Frank Townley, Rod Mackenzie died unexpectedly and was also a great loss to the 'City' Club. For some years he served on the Greens Committee until, in 1973 he was appointed Chairman of that committee.

Rod was not only a low single-figure golfer, but a real thinker about the game and especially about the course layout at the 'City'. He thought there was room for much improvement.

In 1974 he put some of his thoughts on paper for perusal by the members. 'On the whole, we have a reasonable balance of long and short holes, several of which are very good, but one or two are pretty bad' he said. 'We have more acreage than most other comparable clubs but we don't make proper use of it. And, of course, the clubhouse is built in the wrong place'.

Committed to existing greens by the introduction of the 'pop-up' sprinkler system he produced a novel plan of introducing a long par 3 into the corner of the 4th, playing the fifth along the left hand boundary of the present 4th enabling the 17th hole – not the best hole on the course to be closed.

The plan had much merit in that it would cut out the long walks from the 12th to the 13th, and from the 14th to the 15th holes. Under the Mackenzie plan one proceeded from the present 12th green directly to the 16th tee, followed by playing the 15th from a new tee sited to the East of the 16th green. One then followed round to the 14th which would become the new 17th hole, moving on to the 18th tee which would be moved to the north-west so that the drive would be played short of the cross-burn, leaving a long or mid-iron to the last green. Although the plan had much merit, it was never implemented.

Rod Mackenzie will also be remembered for his attempts to improve the scenic layout of the course, introducing a policy of strategically sited tree planting, the purchase of semi-mature trees, and arguing for the transplant of evergreens around certain key greens.

HUGHIE WHITE

The late Hughie White was a popular member of the Club and carried a love for the 'City' Golf Club which he never shouted out loud. This canny Scot was the unknown giver of donations which allowed the greens committee to plant daffodils and other flowers near tee boxes on the 'City' course in the late 1960's. He made his donations on condition that his name was not divulged in his lifetime. In 1973, The General Committee placed on record their appreciation of Hughie's act.

FRANK O'KANE

Frank O'Kane, who joined the 'City' in 1974 has given many years of unstinting service to the Club. For six years, he was an active member of the Greens Committee. Along with one or two other members, Frank has been instrumental in improving the environment and scenic layout of the course, planting the huge total of 1,500 trees or saplings over the years.

The trees at the right hand side of the 1st, on the left of the 15th, along the left of the 17th and behind the 17th green are examples of his handiwork, assisted by George Wilkinson. In various other ways, Frank has introduced attractive features including a water fountain and garden layout in front of the clubhouse.

STAN QUINE

One of the great stalwarts of the 'City' who still played an active part in Club life until a ripe old age was Stan Quine. His reputation as a good golfer preceded his arrival in Newcastle, as he had played for the Yorkshire County Team in the years following World War II. Arriving at our Club in the late 1940's, he began a long and industrious association. He played off 3 handicap for many years, and as age took its toll gradually moved up to 6.

Although he was always a hard man to beat, he found the competition for 'City' trophies in the fifties and sixties (when the club boasted a number of scratch players and very low handicap golfers) intense. He did win several trophies in his 'City' career, including the coveted Pease Coronation Cup after the war.

He made a considerable contribution to the administration side of the club, was a fountain of golfing knowledge and was the man to sort out an argument over the rules. A bluff, dry-humoured man of strong character, Stan was known to often pull a golfer on the spot under Rule 19.

His son, Martin was also a useful low handicap golfer who, after a period as a playing member had to switch to country membership when his job took him outside the area.

THE ELLIOTT FAMILY

Extensive Contribution to Northumberland Golf.

One of the best-known golfing families in Northumberland, which has made a considerable contribution to the game of golf at the City of Newcastle Club, is that of the Elliotts.

Led by the late Gordon Elliott, a former 'City' Captain, he had enthusiastic support from his wife, Iris, herself a past-captain of the 'City G.C.' Ladies.

This extended golfing family included their three children, Frank, Stephen and Barbara, all of whom learned their golf at the Three Mile Bridge and went on to noteworthy achievements in local golf.

By the year 1989 a double honour was accorded Iris and Barbara Elliott when mother and daughter were appointed President and Captain at the same time.

Stephen Elliott was and is the outstanding golfer among the men of the family; he was marked down as a junior of talent when he began at the 'City G.C.' – and gave notice of things to come when he won the Northumberland Junior Stroke Play Championship in 1973.

As he matured, he became a regular member of the 'City G.C.' League Team and carried off numerous trophies. One of his outstanding achievements was to win the 'City G.C.' Club Championship four times from four starts, beginning in 1973.

After moving to Westerhope G.C. towards the end of the 1970's, Stephen achieved a notable triumph in 1979 when he registered a victory in the Northumberland County Championship. 'City G.C.' members who were present at that championship (held at the Three Mile Bridge Course) will recall the inspired striking of the ball by Elliott who unleashed some of the longest driving ever witnessed at the 'City G.C.', (His second shot on the long 17th was a pitching wedge, and he drove the 11th green off the back tee). Other notable wins include the County George Renwick Memorial Medal in 1982.

His father, the late Gordon Elliott, who died suddenly on Boxing Day, 1989 and whose passing was mourned by many, was also a solid golfer himself. His trophies included the Reid Vase in 1966, and the Stuart Trophies twice (1978 and 1980) with his wife, Iris. After moving home to Ponteland, Gordon joined the local golf club, though he retained his links with the 'City G.C.' as a social member. His son, Frank, after marrying Elaine Fraser of the Whitley Bay Club moved there himself. He was elected Captain of that club in 1987.

Elaine Fraser, who became Mrs. Frank Elliott was a success story in her own right: girl international for Scotland, three times County Champion and many times winner of the Club Championship on her own course at Whitley Bay. Barbara, who became Mrs. Ken Wilson cemented a formidable golfing partnership with Ken who made a name for himself with the Newbiggin Golf Club before moving on. In 1974 Ken, a keen league player, was a member of the Newbiggin Team that won the Newcastle and District Golf League Championship, and he later played for the County Team.

In the Ladies Section of the 'City', the records show that the mother-daughter achievements of Iris and Barbara Elliott have been noteworthy. Iris, elected Ladies Captain in 1979 was appointed President in 1989. Her trophies won include the Bronze Trophy three times (1982, 86 and 88), the Larmour Salver in 1972 and the Kent Cup in 1978.

Barbara, a former Ladies Secretary and Ladies Captain in 1989/90 was even more successful on the golf course and is still a formidable player today. Mrs. Wilson has won the Ladies Championship four times (1976, 1981, 1984 and 1991); her other trophies include the Larmour Salver and the Calcutta Cup. In addition, Barbara is a regular league player in a top division.

In 1990, this mother and daughter partnership carried off the County Foursomes for the R.V.I. Cup.

The sporting success of the Elliott family is not unconnected with the career success and love of golf of the late head of the family, Gordon Elliott. A former miner from Dinnington, Northumberland, he left the pits to enter the engineering industry, eventually rising to become head of the firm of mining engineers, R. B. Bolton of Consett. Under his management, the company prospered in the manufacture of mining equipment, building up a considerable export business.

As a result of his achievements in the field of industry he was awarded the M.B.E. during the 1980's.

THOMAS AND GEORGE HARBOTTLE

Golfing Pioneers of the 'City'

The name of Thomas Harbottle may belong to the distant past, but as a founder member of the 'City G.C.' who played for years on the Town Moor, should not be forgotten.

Married with two young sons, Thomas acted for the Weardale Steel, Coke and Coal Company, selling coal for them at the old Newcastle Exchange on the quayside. He began his golfing career in the early 1890's on the advice of his doctor, who told him he was below par and needed fresh air and exercise.

Settling in at the 'City G.C.', his regular partner was a Mr. J. Lang. Later, in 1898 when over 100 'City G.C.' members decided to break away from the 'City' on the Moor, Thomas Harbottle would have nothing to do with it. One serious consideration of refusing to move to 'The Park' was the extra money it would cost him in hiring a horse-cab from his home to reach the Northumberland Club in High Gosforth Park. There was no public transport in those days and the era of the mass-produced automobile had not yet arrived.

When the 'City G.C.' eventually found a new venue at The Three Mile Bridge, he decided after a few years to make both his sons members. One of them, George Harbottle, of Castleton Grove, Jesmond, Newcastle was to become well-known as a local historian and author of 14 books on golf, cricket, local history and poetry.

George, who is approaching a centenary all of his own, being born in the 1890's told the author that one vivid memory of joining the 'City G.C.' was the shock of fees payable. When he joined in 1910 the entrance fee was £10 and the annual subscription was £10. 'That was a great amount of money in those days' he said.

Enjoying his golf at the 'City G.C.', George Harbottle reduced his handicap to 7 before joining up to fight in the Great War. He served with the 6th Battalion of the Northumberland Fusiliers and was commissioned. After the war, he returned to his work on the Newcastle Quayside and The Exchange, and was persuaded by an office colleague to apply to the Northumberland Club. His application was accepted and he began a new golfing career at 'The Park' in the early 1920's.

George Harbottle recalls that after the formation of the 'City G.C.' on the Town Moor, the club's golfers never did wear red jackets, which was the practice at some golf clubs. The reason: the presence of large numbers of cattle grazing close to the fairways!

Two early 'City' characters. The player on the far left was known as 'Pa' to other club members because of his great age. His partner (also shown), a Newcastle solicitor, played in frock coat and floppy cap while smoking a cigar.

Chapter XIV

THE LADIES OF THE 'CITY'

Fine Record Over Many Years

Of the many honours won by lady golfers from the City of Newcastle Golf Club, one stands supreme: the victory in the English Counties Championship when the club's Marie McRae led her team into the record books. Two other members of the 'City' were also part of that national championship win, Valerie Gray and Tina Robinson. While a fourth member of that county team, Elaine Fraser, of Whitley Bay had close links with the 'City'.

During that week in July in 1973 in Berkshire, the standard of play was so high that the county ladies went through the week's battles undefeated. The story is told in full later in this chapter.

Meanwhile, a return to the origins of the 'City' Ladies. Although the present Ladies' Section as we know it was formed in 1925, there were 'City' lady golfers before that. The evidence lies in the club archives where the first mention of ladies is made in the club balance sheet of 1894. Only a handful of ladies had 'dared' tread the links of the original course on the Town Moor; in those far-off days lady members were barely tolerated, and the total annual subscriptions of 1894 of £18 5s bears testimony to their tiny band. It took them four years to secure their own room at the Chimney Mills Clubhouse, as a result of which there was an increase of membership. No early competition books have been unearthed, but there are further entries in the club's minutes until 1906 when the ladies section was disbanded with no reason given.

One can only assume that, like the men golfers on the Town Moor, they became disenchanted with the congestion and encroachment of non-members on the Moor course.

Nearly 20 years and a world war were to venture through the passage of time before the ladies of the 'City' reformed themselves. That day, as recorded in the first minute book to survive was February 2nd, 1925 when 'The Three Mile Ladies' Golf Club' was established. It is true that there were lady golfers at the 'City' when the club started up in 1907 at the Three Mile Bridge, though they were not permitted to form their own section or club. A minute of July 1907 declared that wives, sisters and daughters of members could play the course and enjoy its privileges; all other ladies had to be introduced by a member and had to pay a green fee. Ladies then were not allowed to use the clubhouse except for their own ladies' room. Also, there were severe restrictions on the times they were allowed to play the course.

All that was before 1925 and the formation of the new Ladies Club. At the inaugural meeting at the 'City' were 12 women, one of whom, Miss Robb was invited to take the chair.

The first recorded Ladies' Committee and Officials were:

The 1925 Committee

Captain: Mrs. T. Craig

President: Mrs. Beaumont Pease

Secretary: Miss Robb

Treasurer: Mrs. Bowles

Committee: Mesdames Hudson, Levinson, Craig and Miss Williams.

It was provisionally decided to make the annual subscription 10s 6d.

At the next meeting on May 14th, 1925 the club elected to join the Ladies' Golf Union to take advantage of the universal handicapping system.

Under the rules of the L.G.U. the first competition was held on November 6th when a silver spoon was presented to the winner. To this day the practice of presenting silver spoons has continued, the winners of the monthly medal in both silver and bronze divisions receiving similar awards.

Towards the end of 1926 the new Captain, Mrs. Rooksby rose at the annual meeting, at which 10 members were present, to deplore the fact that few of their members were entering competitions! And while there was a room at the 'City' set aside for lady golfers, they had limited facilities which did not include lockers. At the close of the meeting it was agreed to write to the club committee seeking permission to install lockers at their own expense.

However, just one year later there had been a marked improvement in the fortunes of the ladies. Membership had risen to 40 and 26 lockers had been installed 'to the comfort of members'. By 1928 the ladies' club played only one match in the year, against Hexham, losing 3–5 away and winning 6–2 at home.

By the 1930's the 'City' Ladies began to establish themselves as a powerful force in county golf, and in 1931 won the Northumberland County Bronze Shield. One name that appears frequently in the minutes of this period is that of Miss B. M. Bainbridge. Serving as a committee member for some years and elected Captain in 1931, this lady is almost certainly the Beatrice Bainbridge, daughter of Mrs. Bainbridge who owned and lived in the Grange Farm, the landlord of the 'City' course. In fact, Miss Bainbridge was twice elected Captain.

An early lease agreement between the 'City' and Mrs. Bainbridge stipulated that both her daughters should have free access to the golf course. At least one of them served the Ladies' Club with distinction and was a fine golfer in her own right.

By 1933 the membership had risen to 60 and the finances were in a comparatively healthy state. By 1934, the section showed a profit of £54-1s-6d at the end of the year, a considerable sum in those days.

As the ladies proceeded steadily on, they went from strength to strength although in the 1930's they were very much the 'poor relations' in the 'City' clubhouse, and even on the course.

One outstanding member, Mrs. Hilda Broadbent who joined the club more than 50 years ago has vivid memories of what life was like for the ladies before the

Second World War. 'The men's attitude to women golfers was very stiff' she recalls. One had to know all the rules, both in the club and on the course and stick to them by the letter. 'If one's husband was in the "Men's Only" bar and a wife wanted to communicate, she dare not go anywhere near the entrance door. The only way was to send a message via the steward. There was a glass panel on the door of the men's bar but no lady dare look through it for their husband!' The Professional was not allowed in the clubhouse under any circumstances.

On the course, ladies' matches had to give way to men's matches.

All the lady golfers engaged caddies to play the course. They were mostly pitmen from Hazelrigg and other local pits who reported to the Professional for work during their night-shift week.

A caddy then cost Mrs. Broadbent 1s 1d – one shilling going to the caddy and one penny to the Pro. as booking fee.

On the course, the normal dress was silk blouse with tie plus long woolen skirts and leather-spiked shoes. One of the most popular golf balls of the period was the 'Warwick' which sold at 10d each.

At that time in the Club's history only wives of members or relatives could hope to be accepted as members. Asked if she ever felt bitter about not being accepted as a Club Member in her own right – rather than an Associate which all ladies were – Mrs. Broadbent replied: 'No. When I and others joined the Club more than 50 years ago, we became accustomed to playing a secondary role to men, we just became used to it'.

Before the second World War, Hilda recalls that there were severe restrictions on ladies' starting times. As Monday was the quietest day of the week for the Club, that was declared ladies' competition day. The remainder of the week, ladies could play in mornings only. In the golfing season, play was restricted to mornings and evenings after 6.30 p.m.

'We had a big fight to get more flexible times to cater for our working women golfers' said Mrs. Broadbent.

She can remember clearly the struggle the ladies had to furnish their own hut, which was acquired from the sponsors of the great Newcastle Exhibition of the 1930's. The ladies bought their own furniture and carpets and generated most of their funds by holding bridge drives at 6d a time.

During her career at the 'City', Hilda Broadbent was successful both as an officer of the Ladies' Section and a player. She served on the committee for a period of years, and in 1957 was elected Lady Captain. She played the 'City' Ladies' League Team for many years.

Her trophy wins include the Calcutta, the Bowles and the Captain's Cups. During the 1980's, despite her good age, Hilda was as keen and as competitive as ever, and was still winning during that decade. Her late husband, Harry Broadbent, who died in 1968 was an active member of the 'City' and acknowledged to be a master interpreter of the Rules of Golf.

During the 1930's the City Ladies' Teams made a name for themselves in county golf, and usually held a respectable position in the County Shield.

At the 'City G.C.' Mrs. J. Greenfield won the Cecil Leitch Cup two years in succession which was a Ladies' Match-play competition.

During 1935 there was a significant change in the name of the ladies' club though no reason is given in the official minute dated December 16th, 1935. It merely says: 'Suggested alterations to the constitution of the Ladies' Section were discussed and it was agreed 'to alter the name from the Three Mile Ladies' Golf Club to the City of Newcastle Golf Club (Ladies' Section)'.

The meeting also confirmed that winners of the monthly medals in the summer should receive silver spoons. No spoon was to be given in the four winter months although a 6d sweep would be held. In addition the winners of each division in the winter season would receive 'a 1s 6d ball'.

By 1936 the annual subscriptions for the Ladies' Section was still only 10s 6d. At a committee meeting of February 27th it was decided to give replicas with the trophy presentations.

During these years, the Ladies arranged a number of friendly matches against other clubs including Hexham, Gosforth, Newcastle United and Bellingham.

Another feature of ladies' activities was the holding of picnics in the summer and autumn. In May, 1937 the summer picnic was at Alnmouth, and the Autumn picnic at Otterburn.

There was considerable discussion in 1939 about the position of lady associates who were not members of the Ladies' Club. A minute of January 31st reports the receipt of a letter from the Men's Club Committee trying to rationalise the situation. The letter said that the Club would pay the annual subscription to the L.G.U. together with an additional sum for ladies' section overhead charges if 'all lady associates would automatically become members of the Ladies' Club'. Although they gave no explanation, the ladies' committee rejected the offer. The minute says: 'It was decided that there appeared to be no valid reason why the conditions of the membership of the ladies' club should be altered'.

The outbreak of World War II opened up a trying period for the Ladies' Section of the City of Newcastle Golf Club. The membership stood at 51.

All things considered, the ladies decided that they would try and carry on. Friendly matches were to be held on Tuesday mornings, with the option to make a payment of 6d towards the Red Cross. Members were told that L.G.U. handicaps would be frozen for the duration. Nevertheless, it was agreed to hold competitions in 1940, introducing the awards of club handicaps.

All competition entrance money in 1940 would be sent to the Red Cross.

As the war years dragged on, the ladies' activities were drastically reduced, and did not resume on a proper basis until 1945. The war years had reduced the membership, so perhaps it is not all that surprising to note a reduction in the annual subscription to 8/-.

One good piece of news was that the Ladies' Golf Union had resumed operations. One bad piece of news was the heating in the Ladies' wooden pavilion was practically non-existent, causing much discomfort. Complaints to the club committee seemed to have little effect. The position grew so unacceptable by February 1946, that the Ladies' Committee decided to suspend all home fixtures 'until further notice'. Some action must have been taken as the minute of May 7th, 1946 reports that home and return matches had been arranged with Morpeth and Whitley Bay clubs.

It was noticeable that by 1947, the ladies had been successful in relaxing the stiff restrictions on their playing times. The minute of June 21st reads: 'A proposal was made by Mrs. Nicholson and seconded by Mrs. Smith – and the committee agreed – that in future players may tee off at any time in Medal rounds and all Friday competitions.'

The year 1947 also saw a solution to the problem of lady associates and club membership which had first been raised eight years before. The Ladies' Committee decided that those who paid an annual green fee should be allowed to join the Ladies' Club, and to play under a club handicap. They were, however, disqualified from playing in monthly medal and trophy competitions where an L.G.U. handicap applied.

Steady progress was made in these difficult post-war years, with food and clothes rationing and the production of golf equipment not back into full swing. The ladies competed on a team, and individual basis, with a certain measure of success. At a time when the City of Newcastle was feeling the post-war pinch, the ladies were always organising events to raise money and help out.

In 1957, when a new Professional, Sam McRae, was appointed to serve the City of Newcastle G.C. he brought with him a lady who was destined to make a name for herself in ladies' golf – Marie McRae, his wife.

Strangely, when Marie arrived in Newcastle from Silloth she had never played a round of golf in her life. Walking on the 'City' course must have inspired her as she told her husband she had got the bug. Sam, the professional planned her golfing career in meticulous fashion. For a whole year, she did nothing but swing a golf club – either in the garden or on a mat indoors under the guiding and watchful eye of her husband.

One fine day, it was agreed that she was ready to make her debut on the 'City'. Marie will not forget the first shot she hit in golf. 'Sam handed me a 5 iron and said "Hit through that". I struck the ball and it soared away down the middle'. She said 'That was it, I had got the golfing bug'. That grooved, silky swing has remained with her ever since, so there's a lesson for beginners. In fact Marie still loves the feel of a golf club, even away from the course. 'I can still get great pleasure from swinging a golf club, and I often do' she said.

Although Marie McRae did not start to play until she was over 30, she has won practically every local golf honour in sight during her career. For example she has won the City Ladies' Club Championship 18 times. Her form was such one year that so few golfers entered the club championship that it had to be cancelled with Marie as defending champion. She has been Captain, President and Vice-President of the City Ladies. A recent honour was to be asked by the County to become a Northumberland Vice-President.

Even the mighty must occasionally take a fall. The incident resulted in Marie becoming one of the few lady members to take a bath in the Ouseburn which runs across the first fairway. It happened some years ago when she was playing with Yvonne Kent. When Yvonne's second shot fell into the burn, Marie grasped on to a low branch of a tree to try to retrieve the ball. The branch gave away and plunged her unceremoniously head-first into the cooling waters!

In a long, glorious golfing career there can be no argument about her proudest achievement. It was leading the Northumberland Ladies' Team to victory in the English Counties finals in 1973.

Looking back, Marie recalls the tremendous team spirit that prevailed that year. That did not happen by accident. Marie had worked out a master-plan of preparation for the event.

It was so extensive that it could not have been done without the co-operation of many golf clubs in Northumberland. 'Basically, I arranged a series of matches against male county players, playing off back-tees at different courses under different weather conditions. By the time the championships came around, natural talent had become match-hardened' she said.

Marie was drawing on much experience of county play. She had represented Northumberland for some years. Another plus was that playing the key role of county coach was her husband, Sam McRae.

There was another 'City' link with this triumphant victory – included in the county team were two young golfers, Valerie Gray and Tina Robinson, both of the City of Newcastle G.C. While another team member, Elaine Fraser of Whitley Bay was a member of the 'City' Ladies' Section for two seasons at the beginning of the 1970's.

The full team representing Northumberland County in that memorable win of 1973 was: Marie McRae (Captain); Tric Todd (Vice-Captain); Jennie Lee-Smith (Gosforth); Margaret Pickard (Alnmouth); Valerie Stone (Morpeth); Audrey Pattison (Morpeth); Penny Nelson (Alnmouth); Elaine Fraser (Whitley Bay); Valerie Gray and Tina Robinson (City of Newcastle).

In that English Ladies' Championship week's golf, the Northumberland squad came through undefeated, beating Warwickshire in the final. The road to victory had been prepared when Northumberland earlier beat the might of the North of England at the Northumberland Club. After emerging victorious in the English County Finals, Captain McRae told the Press: 'I felt from the start that we were all in form and that we were going to win. I'm so proud of them'.

Back home in Newcastle with the national trophy, Marie McRae stated: 'What I did for Northumberland County was a reflected honour for the 'City' Club, I always felt that'.

Subsequent to that glorious victory, one member of the county team accepted the challenge of turning professional, and was soon to make a name for herself. Foremost among the professional successes of Jennie Lee-Smith was winning the Ladies' British Open Championship.

The Ladies' Section has been fortunate over the years in enlisting long-serving members who were also prepared to help the Club. The late Nancy Balfour – who joined the 'City' prior to World War II as a teenager – had been the longest-serving member along with Hilda Broadbent.

One outstanding character of The Ladies was the late Margaret Ferris who left a fine record of service to the club. A former Captain and then Ladies' Treasurer, Margaret came into her own when she was appointed Secretary, a post she held for many years. While she may have been a stickler for the rules, she organised ladies' competitions and other events with efficiency and great accomplishment.

Although Margaret played the game during the season (she put her clubs away every October until the following April), and won more than one trophy in her golfing career, her heart lay in golf organisation at which she excelled. Once she had given a ruling, there was no shifting her. Joining the 'City' from the Bridle Patch Club, Margaret was connected with the 'City' for some 40 years. In addition, she had served on the Northumberland County Veterans' Committee.

One member who often played with Margaret was Freda Foster, who joined the Ladies' Section more than 30 years ago, and was elected Captain in 1972. Freda, with her husband Bill Foster, hold what may be a unique record in North-East golf: together, they have been connected with the game for a total of 100 years or more.

Freda started to play at Crook G.C. as a young woman, moving on to Consett and Bishop Auckland before joining the 'City' in 1959. Bill joined the Consett Club in 1937, moving to Bishop Auckland ten years later before joining the City of Newcastle Club.

Freda's honours include wins in the Captain's and President's Days, the Calcutta Cup and three L.G.U. Silver Medals for best season's aggregate.

When Esme Duncan joined the Ladies' Section of the 'City G.C.' in 1961 she could hardly have foreseen the major role that the Duncan family was to play in the life of the Club. In the 30 or so years that Esme has been a member she has served as Ladies' Captain, Ladies' Secretary, Committee member and also as a member of the Club Centenary Committee.

In 1981 Esme Duncan broke new ground when she accepted an invitation to become full Club Secretary at the City Golf Club – the first woman at the 'City' to hold such office.

She did not accept the post without some trepidation: would there be raised eyebrows from senior club members used to dealing with a mere male? In the event, there was no opposition to the appointment. Mrs. Duncan held that office until 1986 when she decided to step down.

On the field of play, the years 1978 and 1979 were meritorious landmarks for the 'City G.C.' Lady League players. They won the Ladies' County Association 'B' Division Championship in 1978, and the following year carried all before them to lift the 'A' Division Championship

Looking back at the history of the Ladies' Section at the City of Newcastle Golf Club, one can only conclude that the Club would have been a poorer place without them. Apart from their successes in county competition, the ladies have been great fundraisers for the Club over the years.

Ladies Section

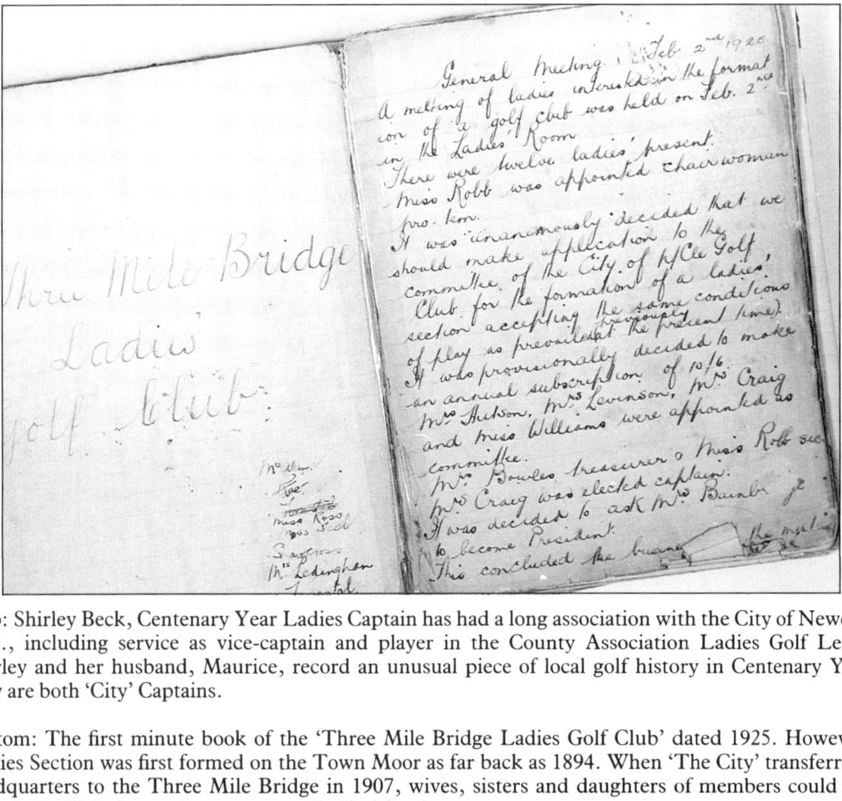

Three Mile Bridge Ladies' Golf Club

General Meeting Feb 2nd 192[illegible]

A meeting of ladies interested in the formation of a golf club was held on Feb. 2nd in the Ladies' Room

There were twelve ladies present.

Miss Robb was appointed chairwoman pro. tem.

It was unanimously decided that we should make application to the committee of the City of N/Cle Golf Club for the formation of a ladies' section accepting the same conditions of play as prevailed at the present time.

It was provisionally decided to make an annual subscription of 10/6.

Mrs Aitkson, Mrs Levinson, Mrs Craig and Miss Williams were appointed as committee.

Mrs Bowles treasurer & Miss Robb sec

Mrs Craig was elected captain.

It was decided to ask Mrs [illegible] to become President.

This concluded the business [illegible]

Top: Shirley Beck, Centenary Year Ladies Captain has had a long association with the City of Newcastle G.C., including service as vice-captain and player in the County Association Ladies Golf League. Shirley and her husband, Maurice, record an unusual piece of local golf history in Centenary Year – they are both 'City' Captains.

Bottom: The first minute book of the 'Three Mile Bridge Ladies Golf Club' dated 1925. However, a Ladies Section was first formed on the Town Moor as far back as 1894. When 'The City' transferred its headquarters to the Three Mile Bridge in 1907, wives, sisters and daughters of members could play, though the Club frowned on a separate Ladies' Section.

Top: Margaret Finkle, Ladies' President for 1990/91 who is also a former Ladies' Captain. Pictured here with Northumberland County Past Captains Trophies won with the late Nancy Balfour.

Bottom: During the 1990 season a mother and daughter partnership landed a premier trophy for 'the City'. Mrs. Barbara Wilson (left) holds the R.V.I. Cup for the County Foursomes with mother, Mrs. Iris Elliott (last won by the club in 1933).

Top: Several 'City' lady golfers were associated with the outstanding achievement of Northumberland winning the All-England County Championship of 1973. The County Captain was Marie McRae (wife of Sam McRae) and the team also included Valerie Gray and Tina Robinson from 'The City'.

Bottom: A powerful ladies quartet from the Three Mile Bridge who won the County Ladies Golf Association team event in 1975. L. to R: Valerie Gray, Bea Taylor, Marie McRae and Ann Robinson.

Top: The leading 'City' Ladies League Team of 1991, competing in Division 2 of the County Association.
Back row, L. to R: Ashleigh Easton, Janette Fellows, Jessica Gore-Sellon, Marie McRae and Barbara Wilson.
Front, L. to R: Ann Parkinson, Lesley Wheeler, Oliver Slater (Capt.) and Rosalie Hunter.

Bottom: The second Ladies League Team for 1991, competing in Division 5.
Back row, L. to R: Shirley Beck (Vice-Capt. when picture taken) Vivienne Brown, Iris Elliott, Dorothy Wark and Joan Smith.
Front, L. to R: Joyce Hargreaves, Rosemary Smith, Esme Duncan and Isobel Johnstone.

Top: The Ladies Committee 1990/91:
Front row, L. to R: Esme Duncan (Secretary), Olive Slater, (Capt.) Shirley Beck, Joyce Alexander (Treasurer).
Back row: Joan Davison, Audrey Croft, Janette Fellows, Rosemary Smith, Ann Crosby, Pamela Leigh and Ann Parkinson.

Bottom: A Ladies Captain's Day group in 1985.
Front row, L. to R: Lilian Mason, Sheila Tennant (Capt.), Joyce Alexander, Joyce Hargreaves and Joan Dawe (President).
Back: Lorna Sleight, Betty Welsh, Irene Atkinson, Doreen Robinson, Dorothy Wark, 'Dolly' Jordan and Rosalie Hunter.

Chapter XV

HOW THE 'CITY' JUNIORS BECAME A FORCE

League Players in the Making

Only in the last decade and a half have the junior golfers of the 'City G.C.' been moulded and organised into a golfing force, capable of holding its own with any team in the county.

Before 1977 – the first time the 'City' competed in the Northumberland Junior League – the Club possessed keen young golfers who mostly confined their competition entries to Club events. In the early 1970's the Junior Section at the 'City G.C.' included John Gibson, Robin Sleight, Ian and Andrew McKinna, David Nicholson, Chris Wood, Robin Davison, Tony Hannington, Frank and Stephen Elliott.

There had been some success at county level by individuals: Stephen Elliott won the County Junior Stroke Play Championship in 1973, and nearly 10 years before that Brian White won the same event back-to-back (1964 and 1965).

Though it was due mainly to the initiative of John Blackburn that the talent of the 'City G.C.' Juniors was honed into a golfing force. After Mr. Blackburn was elected to the Club Committee in 1976 he successfully argued for the Club to enter teams at junior county level.

After some debate, and with the help of members like Arthur Smith and Michael Wilkes the League Team was formed.

As often happens when the fledglings leave the nest for the first time, they encounter hard and unrelenting forces which threaten to strike them down. That first season in league golf was a baptism of fire for the 'City' Junior Team. They went down 12–0 in the inaugural game, and went on to lose most other matches during the season.

Compared with other teams in the league, the 'City' discovered that the ages of their players were considerably lower, while their handicaps were higher.

The first team, playing away to Bedlington on a cold and windy day in 1977 was K. Gill (aged 14 years), M. Sellers (16), P. Smith (15), I. Matthewson (13), P. Tennant (14) and M. Blackburn (12).

Although it was going to take some time for the 'City' to make its presence felt in this county league, it says much for committee members like John Blackburn, Arthur Smith, Michael Wilkes, Miles Watson, Colin Hewitt, Bill Smith and Ian McIntosh that they stuck with the challenge over a period of years.

The Liaison Officer for the Junior Team in 1991 is Colin Hewitt, assisted by Chris Miller.

Top: A piece of junior golf history at 'The City'. Pictured is the first Northumberland Junior League Squad in 1977.
Back row, L. to R: M. Grant, M. Blackburn, K. Gill, S. Custis, P. Tennant, C. Mason, John Blackburn (Team Organiser) and I. Matthewson.
Middle: D. Miller, C. Miller and S. Smith. Front: I. Duncan and G. Duncan.

Bottom: 'The City' Junior League Team, 1991.
L. to R: Steven Leigh, Alan Scott, Mark Bidetta, Chris Miller (Asst. Liaison Officer), Neil O'Hara (Capt.), Geoffrey May, David Duncan, and Martin Gray.

The rewards for training and practice coupled with the acquisition of experience at county level showed itself in the 1980's when the 'City' Juniors went agonisingly close to winning the Northumberland Title (in 1986.) After going down away to Prudhoe (8–4) in the opening match, the 'City' hardly looked back, winning five of their next 13 matches by the maximum of 12–0!

In the end, the 'City' were pipped at the post by Prudhoe, losing the county championship by only two points. This was an excellent team performance sustained over a long period, and will retain golden memories for the 'City' Squad. Incidentally, the clock had turned full circle in the encounters with Bedlington since that first drubbing in 1977. In 1986 the 'City' reversed that earlier thrashing, beating Bedlington 12–0.

Members of the 'City' Squad were: David Shepherd (Capt.), Graeme Taylor, Neil Custis, David Smith, David Duncan, Phillip Warren, John Watson, Julian Pearson, Darren Varley, Andrew Moffat and Gary Scott.

The improvement in the standard of play in the 1980's was very considerable, resulting in handicaps tumbling down. For instance in the successful 1986 season Captain David Shepherd was playing off 8 handicap, while Neil Custis, Graeme Taylor and David Smith were all playing off 9.

In 1987, the 'City' Juniors retained the Railton Cup for Target Golf, defeating Newcastle United in a group play-off. The team: David Shepherd, David Smith and David Duncan.

Apart from a higher standard of play, competing at county level also helped attitudes and etiquette, as well as stimulating much more interest in their golfing prowess from club members. One result of that has been the donation of trophies by members for junior competition. The trophies include the Harry Hann Tankard, the Sid Gradwell Shield, the David Moffat Tankard, the Neil Custis Trophy and the John Blackburn Match-play Cup.

John Blackburn also came up with the idea some years ago of staging a Father and Son (or Daughter) Competition, bringing more parents into play with their off-spring. This annual event has proved extremely popular. After Arthur and Peter Smith won the first competition, Michael Wilkes donated two trophies for future 'Father and Son' events.

Another reward to accrue from the increased standards of junior golf at the 'City' has been the elevation of former junior members to the senior 'City' League team, to compete in the Newcastle and District League. Former juniors who have either played regularly for the 'City' League team in the past, or who are still representing the 'City' at present include: Stephen Elliott, Ian McKinna, Robin Sleight, Michael Blackburn, Peter Smith, Ian Matthewson, Chris Mason, Ken Cairns, David Shepherd and Robin Davison.

Anthony Matthew, Professional, City of Newcastle G.C. He arrived at the 'City' from Stowmarket in 1982. After four years with the club, he figured in a new chapter of 'city' history when he became the first to undertake the duties of Professional and Club Secretary.

Chapter XVI

THE 'CITY' PROFESSIONALS

The late Henry Longhirst, intrepid golfer, the 'father' of Television commentators on the golf game and outstanding journalist once wrote: 'Many club golfers, pre-occupied with the daily frustrations of life and seeking no more from their golf than week-end relaxation, are inclined to accept the Pro. as something that goes with the club. Like the poor, he is always with us.'

However true that remains today, one thing is certain – the life of the club Professional has greatly changed since the first Pro. was appointed by the 'City G.C.' in 1891. In order to survive in the 1990's, the Club Pro. needs a shrewd business head as well as a good golfing brain.

Life and making a living was not easy for the first Professional of the City of Newcastle Golf Club when he took up his duties on the Town Moor in October, 1891. His retainer was £52 per annum, a pound per week, which meant that in order to make a real living he had to be skilled at club-making, as well as club-repairing. The majority of his extra income came from that, plus monies received for giving lessons.

Tom Fernie, from Ardeer, Scotland, who was the first Professional stayed a few years and then resigned the position. He was succeeded by John Summerville who also left the Club after a comparatively short time.

The first Professional to make the 'City' his home for a long period was J. S. Caird. Described by his contemporaries as a very competent golfer rather than an outstanding player, Mr. Caird was, nevertheless a man of great knowledge about the game and an excellent teacher. It was he who taught the secrets of golf to Douglas Edgar, the finest professional golfer to emerge from these parts.

J. S. Caird himself played some of the golfing masters of the day and was never disgraced, though the great Harry Vardon always beat him by a handful of shots. This 'City' professional, after working for the Club for a decade on the Town Moor moved with the Club in 1907 to the Three Mile Bridge, giving valuable support to Vardon when he laid out the new course.

While professional on the Moor, Mr. Caird was approached by the Northumberland Golf Club to assist in the preparation of their new course in 1898 which he did. Among other help, it was the 'City' Pro. who decided the location of the original tees. Indeed, Mr. Caird was so accomplished that he was invited by 'The Park' to become Professional at their club.

It was an offer that he declined.

In all, J. S. Caird gave 23 years of loyal and devoted service to the 'City' from which the Club greatly benefited. Remaining with the Club until the end of the 1914–18 War, he then accepted an offer to become Professional to the Hexham Club.

Sam McRae, the longest serving Professional at the 'City' G.C. He was appointed in 1957 from Silloth G.C. and ran the Pro's Shop for 24 years. Always immaculately turned out, he was an engaging character in his own right. He died in 1991.

The next Professional to arrive on the scene was Andrew Kay. Described as 'a very capable golfer but not particularly good at either teaching or club-making', he only stayed for two years.

His successor was Cyril Fryer, something of a character, a tall no-nonsense Scot who had an extensive knowledge of the game, course lay-out and equipment. His advertisements read: 'Golf clubs, singly or in sets, made to order and sent to any part of the world'. Always dressed in plus fours and tweed jacket, he liked things 'ship-shape and Bristol Fashion' supervising caddies and course staff with the air of the benevolent headmaster. His prowess as a teacher was well-known; and he was also a canny golfer winning several championships in the 1920's, including that of North Lancashire, Cumberland and Westmorland. In 1930, he left to take up a post with Hesketh G.C., Southport.

His successor, James Fryer also turned out to be a fine servant of the Club remaining as Professsional until 1947, a total of 17 years' service. His popularity with the City of Newcastle G.C. was reflected in the Club Committee decision to give him the courtesy of the course and the Club at any time.

By 1948 when the new Professional, Robert M. Sandow was appointed the retaining fee paid to him was £150.00 per annum.

After comparatively short service to the Club, he left in mysterious circumstances. Without any notice given or intimation of imminent departure, he vanished over-night! Eventually, it was discovered that he had emigrated to Switzerland, picking up a job at Lucerne Golf Club.

Another namesake, L. H. Sandow was appointed temporary professional while the club committee deliberated. In 1949 they appointed Jack Armitage to the professional berth, but he resigned in 1951 to become Pro. at Temple Newsham.

The next Professional to be engaged was Eric J. Wallis from was appointed from Brighton and Hove G.C. in 1952. He remained in the post until 1957 when another canny Scot, Sam McRae was appointed from Silloth G.C.

This association was to turn out to be a long-lasting one, in which Sam set up the record for long service by a professional, notching up 24 years at the 'City G.C'.

When Mr. McRae arrived in Newcastle, more than 30 years ago, some golfers were still asking to engage caddies. The fee for 18 holes was 2s 6d for a caddie of experience and 1s 6d for a boy caddie.

Golf balls were cheap to buy, every golf ball was separately wrapped. The most popular balls were the 'Warwick' at one shilling and the 'Dunlop 65' at one shilling and sixpence. He recalled that four-ball matches at the 'City' liked to play each other 'for a wrapped ball'.

Over the years, the most common request to him was 'How can you get me to hit the ball further?' Another common fault discussed was the slice. Sam McRae, an excellent teacher could pick out a golfer's fault in a flash and put him, or her, right. Top county players would come to him to iron out a fault. When the County Ladies won the English Championship in 1973, the coach to the winning team was Mr. McRae. One of the biggest compliments paid to him was from a low handicap man from London years ago.

The Londoner, paying a visit to the 'City' course and labouring under a major fault went to Sam for advice. After Sam had discovered the trouble, effecting a cure that very day, the visitor came up to Newcastle for annual lessons for some years afterwards.

Sam was a character in his own right, always immaculately turned out with plus fours or plus twos with jacket to match, not to mention like stockings inside shining leather shoes.

Some would say that he was a 'canny' businessman though he was always good company and could regale members with an unlimited supply of jokes and entertaining stories. He had a deep understanding of the aura surrounding the world of golf and was a master craftsman and technician when it came to making or repairing a golf club.

One Captain of the 'City' said of him: 'Sam had such a magnificent pair of hands as well as the technical skill to tackle any golf club deficiency'. In the 1950's, 1960's and 1970's the small workshop attached to the Professional's hut was a wonder to behold for the aficionados of golf.

Inside, one could find the craftsman at work, like the bespoke tailor fashioning a fine garment, he could be glimpsed varnishing a beautifully fashioned club-head after joining steel shaft with surgical skill, weaving the neat binding at some speed without leaving a knot. The whole operation carried out in the unique, miscellaneous aroma of wood shavings, twine, leather and hot glue; with countless golf tools and instruments hung in good order and ready for instant use.

For many people bitten by the golf bug and fascinated by the implements of the game, a visit to 'Sam's Workshop' was something to be remembered and treasured.

Although it seems incredible, Mr. McRae's golfing career began at the age of 5 years. His father, a Scot, gave him a cut down 'mashie' (name for an old, hickory-shafted iron) and said, 'Sam my boy, when you can play that one, I'll give you another'. I suppose that was a canny Scot's way of introducing his son to the game of golf, though naturally it took time for young Sam to acquire a whole set. Applying himself to the game, he became a very good player by the time he reached his early twenties, was chosen to represent Scotland in an amateur international.

Running parallel with his love for golf was a yearning to join the theatre and the world of entertainment. First he became a professional ice-skater, then a musician, ukelele player and entertainer making theatre appearances as well as broadcasts for B.B.C. Radio. He landed a part in one of the hit musicals of the day in London's West End, 'Sonny', starring Jack Buchanan and Binnie Hale, two big names in the theatre of the 1930's.

In the end – although he had been removed from the game for long periods – he returned to his first love, the game of golf. In 1951 he was appointed Club Master at Cadder Golf Club, near Glasgow, moving on to the championship club of Silloth, before he accepted the Professional's job at the 'City' in 1957.

In all the years he has been connected with the game, one of the major changes witnessed has been the improving standards of the young golfers. 'They are much more mature, and the explosion in coaching through schools and the Sports Council has paid handsome dividends' he said. Sam always took a delight in teaching young golfers himself. And during his stay at the 'City' he was invited to make a number of films for Tyne Tees Television, illustrating his approach to playing some of the most unusual and difficult golf holes on North-East courses.

The lasting portrait of Sam McRae is that of the fine old Pro., always smartly dressed in his plus fours, tartans or tweeds with a quip or two for all members and a wealth of golfing stories at the ready.

This story reflects the impact Sam McRae made on visitors from overseas. It was not unusual for American visitors to the course to compliment him on his turn out, particularly on his selection of plus fours and plus twos. One day an American golfer said to Sam in his shop: 'I admire your knickers – I've got to have a pair like that to take back to the United States'. Sam replied that was the only pair he had with him. Pressed to sell, Sam dashed home, picked up another pair returned to the shop and sold them at a nice price, much to the delight of the Yankee!

Peter Harrison, who succeeded Sam McRae on his retirement in 1981 was a good professional golfer who was keen to compete on the professional circuit. Although he soon settled in and was popular with members, the urge to launch himself onto the Professional tour did not lessen.

When he was unable to reach agreement about a change of terms with the club, he left. Subsequently, Peter won his professional tour card, and has turned in some creditable performances over the years.

It was in 1982 that our current Professional, Anthony Matthew was appointed by the Club. He arrived from Stow Market G.C. where he had been assistant professional to Chris Aldridge. Though it was a stroke of fortune that brought Anthony to the North-East in the first place. In 1980 he travelled North to compete in the 'Newcastle 900 Tournament', playing the qualifying round at the 'City' before competing in the finals at the Northumberland Club.

After four years as 'City' Professional, he figured in a little bit of club history; for the first time in nearly 100 years the Club decided to combine the posts of Professional and Club Secretary. That arrangement has already lasted five years.

Anthony caught the golf 'bug' at an early age and when he was 13, playing out of Mannings Heath G.C., Horsham (Sussex) he won the 'Daily Telegraph' Tournament for Juniors with a nett 65. Incredibly, it was only his third round of golf.

His zest for the game fired him into turning professional at the age of 16, securing his first berth as a junior assistant to Tommy Horton at Ham Manor G.C. Also attached to Ham Manor was Sam Torrance.

In 1975 Anthony Matthew moved to Stoke-by-Nayland, Colchester. Then in 1979 he departed to become Assistant Pro. at Stow Market G.C. where he learned the real business of a club Pro's life – the economics of running a shop.

His golfing career wins include numerous Pro-Am's; at the age of 23 he was runner-up in the Midlands Assistants Championship; while some years ago he shot a 66 in a professional event at Southwold Golf Club to establish a new course record.

How the scoring has come tumbling down over the years. The first course record entered in the Minute Books of the 'City G.C.' was a score of 83: out in 44, back in 39, over the Town Moor course on May 25th, 1892 by Tom Fernie, Professional.

The Northumberland Senior League Squad, 1991.
Front row, L. to R: John Sleight, Jim Browning, Frank O'Kane, Bill Elder (Secretary and Organiser), Norman Finkle and Jim Slater.
Middle: Lou Carr, Norman Atkinson, Billy Greenhalgh, Bill Tennant, Eric Tilney, Malcolm Reed, Tom Birbeck and John Wark.
Back: Lou Edwards, Eric Mason, Gerry Miller, Ken Ridley, Dennis Poole, Pat Pepper and Ron Emens.

Chapter XVII

THE COUNTY SENIOR MEMBERS LEAGUE

'City G.C.' Founder Member

The introduction of the Northumberland Senior Members Golf League in 1974 turned out to be a boon for many of the older members of the club, providing friendly but challenging competition against other county clubs in the summer months.

When the idea was launched in March, 1974 by Peter Donald of Gosforth G.C., an approach was made to the 'City G.C.' to join. It was due mainly to the initiative of one man, the late Gwynne Jones that the 'City G.C.' was not left out in the cold.

For after receiving an invitation to join the new league, the 'City G.C.' turned it down. The club secretary informed Mr. Donald: 'Your letter with preliminary details has been in front of the committee. It was subsequently exhibited on our notice board for a period of two weeks. Insufficient support was received, and as a consequence it has been decided not to proceed further with your suggestion'.

Thanks to the efforts of Gwynne Jones, helped by the late Rod McKenzie who enthused senior members, the 'City G.C.' Committee was persuaded to change its mind, an application was re-submitted and approved by the managers of the new league. The 'City G.C.' agreed that league teams of eight plus four reserves play matches at the Three Mile Bridge under the rules of the NSMGL.

So, some 17 years ago the City of Newcastle G.C. entered this county venture with nine other Northumberland clubs, and it is no exaggeration to say that it has been an unqualified success. So much so that one or two golf clubs who elected not to join the League on its formation have lived to regret it.

As the League prospered over the years, Gwynne was justly rewarded. He was elected President of the Senior League as well as an Hon. Member of the City Golf Club Section.

In the Articles of Association of the League, one clause states: 'The object of this League is to bring those members of an age together to enjoy competitive golf, and the pleasure of meeting old friends in pleasant surroundings'. The tenets of this guide-line have been followed to the letter by the 'City G.C.'; every member of the Senior Section can play in the League. Even so, after the completion of the 1990 season the 'City G.C.' finished in sixth position. The smooth running of League events at the 'City G.C.' following the retirement of Gwynne Jones has been due entirely to the efforts of Bill Elder, assisted by Frank O'Kane.

Acknowledgements
and Thanks

The Editor, 'Evening Chronicle', Newcastle upon Tyne.
The Royal and Ancient Golf Club of St. Andrews.
Frank Manders and Staff of the Local History Department,
Newcastle City Library.
Staff of Tyne and Wear Archives, Newcastle upon Tyne.
University of Newcastle Library.
Northumberland Records Office.
Thomas Ball of Fenham, Newcastle upon Tyne.
Newcastle Daily Journal – 1892.
Kelly's Directory – 1906.
'The Sporting Man' – 1907.
The 'Golfing Annual' Edited by D. S. Duncan – 1908.
'The Sporting Chronicle'.
'The Quayside Golfing Society' and 'The Northumberland Golf Story'
by George Harbottle.
'The Gate to Golf' by J. Douglas Edgar.
'The City of Newcastle G.C. Handbook by Ken McKenzie – 1966.
Dudley Hallwood – Cartoonist.

The author would also like to express thanks to the men and women of the City of Newcastle G.C. who gave their time to relate memories, anecdotes and experiences, and especially to the following: John Boyd, Norman Finkle, Bill Balfour, Miles Watson, David Moffat, David Beardall, John Duncan, John Blackburn, Norman Dodds, Colin Hewitt, Joe Steele and Bill Elder.

From the Ladies: Esme Duncan, Hilda Broadbent, Freda Foster and Marie McRae.

The Appendix

CLUB HONOURS 1909–1959

1909	County Championship	N. R. E. Wilkinson	
	County Club Championship	J. C. Seymour	N. R. E. Wilkinson
		G. Atkinson	P. Forsyth Jnr.
1911	County Championship	N. R. E. Wilkinson	
	County Club Championship	J. C. Seymour	N. R. E. Wilkinson
		G. Atkinson	P. Forsyth Jnr.
1923	County Club Championship	P. Forsyth Jnr.	E. Sullivan
		W. F. Curtis	C. W. Howie
1924	County Championship	C. W. Howie	
1927	County Championship	R. E. Gray	
1929	Chronicle Cup	E. Sullivan	R. E. Gray
1930	County Club Championship	E. Sullivan	R. E. Gray
		C. W. Howie	T. B. Colpitts
1931	Chronicle Cup	E. Sullivan	R. E. Gray
	County Club Championship	E. Sullivan	R. E. Gray
		T. B. Colpitts	T. Greenfield
1933	County Club Championship	E. Sullivan	R. E. Gray
		G. Boswell	N. Weatherston
1934	County Championship	R. E. Gray	
1935	Chronicle Cup	R. E. Gray	E. Sullivan
1939	Chronicle Cup	G Boswell	A. C. Moffat
	County Championship	R. E. Gray	
1946	County Club Championship	A. Black	P. Richardson
		E. Sullivan	R. E. Gray
	County Championship	R. E. Gray	
1947	Chronicle Cup	R. E. Gray	P. Richardson
1950	County Championship	W. B. Blake	
1951	County Club Championship	W. B. Blake	G. M. Cairns
		R. E. Gray	H. W. Hindmarsh
1954	Chronicle Cup	R. E. Gray	H. W. Hindmarsh
1955	George Renwick Medal	D. Moffat	
1956	George Renwick Medal	D. Moffat	
	Chronicle Cup	R. E. Gray	D. Moffat
1957	George Renwick Medal	D. Moffat	
	County Club Championship	R. E. Gray	H. W. Hindmarsh
		D. Moffat	G. C. Wilkinson
1958	English International	D. Moffat	
1958	County Club Championship	D. Moffat	R. E. Gray
		G. C. Wilkinson	J. F. Duncan
	County Championship	D. Moffat	
1959	Inter-County Foursomes	D. Moffat	R. E. Gray

Honours
DAVID MOFFAT

1954	Boy International
1955	George Renwick Medal
	Youth International
1956	George Renwick Medal
1957	George Renwick Medal
	Youth International
1958	Northumberland Amateur Champion
	Youth International and Captain
1959	Northumberland Amateur Champion
	Northumberland and Durham Open
	English International
1960	English International
1961	Northumberland Amateur Champion
	English International
	European Teams Championship
1963	Northumberland 72 Hole Stroke Play Champion
	English International
	European Teams Championship
1964	Golf Illustrated Gold Vase
	Northumberland 72 Hole Stroke Play Champion
1965	English International
	Inter-County Foursomes (D. Moffat and F. Cowley)
1967	Northumberland Amateur Champion
	English International
1969	Northumberland Amateur Champion
	Northumberland and Durham Open
1975	Northumberland and Durham Open
1976	Northumberland and Durham Stroke Play
1977	Northumberland County Captain
1985	English Boys Selector
1985–86	Northumberland County Captain

YEAR	CAPTAIN	PRESIDENT	CLUB CHAMPION
1891	Dr. Adam Wilson	J. W. Pease	
1892	J. B. Pease	J. W. Pease	J. B. Pease
1893	R. T. Thompson	J. W. Pease	
1894	J. B. Radcliffe	J. W. Pease	
1895	J. B. Radcliffe	J. W. Pease	
1896	W. R. Rumbold	J. W. Pease	
1897	Rev. D. I. Ritchie	J. W. Pease	
1898	J. B. Radcliffe	J. W. Pease	
1899	F. E. Thew	J. W. Pease	
1900	F. E. Thew	J. W. Pease	
1901	F. E. Thew	J. W. Pease	
1902	F. E. Thew	J. B. Pease	
1903	Jos. Miller	J. B. Pease	
1904	Jos. Miller	J. B. Pease	Surviving records
1905	A. Cameron	J. B. Pease	re-commence from
1906	J. Bolam	J. B. Pease	1936
NEW COURSE			
1907	J. Bolam	J. B. Pease	
1908	J. T. Gracie	J. B. Pease	
1909	J. T. Gracie	J. B. Pease	
1910	J. C. Seymour	J. B. Pease	
1911	P. Forsyth Jnr.	J. B. Pease	
1912	J. O. Morgan	J. B. Pease	
1913	J. M. Kent	J. B. Pease	
1914	C. H. Watson	J. B. Pease	
1915	J. T. Ferguson	J. B. Pease	
1916	J. T. Ferguson	J. B. Pease	World War I
1917	J. T. Ferguson	J. B. Pease	1914–1918
1918	J. T. Ferguson	J. B. Pease	
1919	P. Forsyth Jnr.	J. B. Pease	
1920	W. A. Poulis	J. B. Pease	
1921	W. F. Curtis	J. B. Pease	
1922	W. J. Lockerby	J. B. Pease	
1923	W. Forsyth	J. B. Pease	
1924	C. W. Howie	J. B. Pease	
1925	E. Fogg	J. B. Pease	
1926	W. H. Dempster	J. B. Pease	
1927	S. Jones	J. B. Pease	
1928	S. Jones	J. B. Pease	
1929	R. G. Kirkby	J. B. Pease	
1930	R. G. Kirkby	J. B. Pease	
1931	R. B. Cairns	J. B. Pease	

YEAR	CAPTAIN	PRESIDENT	CLUB CHAMPION
1932	J. H. Boyd	Sir Stephen Easten	
1933	T. R. Jackson	Sir Stephen Easten	
1934	W. B. Taylor	Sir Stephen Easten	
1935	W. B. Taylor	Sir Stephen Easten	
1936	E. Sullivan	Sir Stephen Easten	R. E. Gray
1937	H. I. Higginbottom	Sir Stephen Easten	E. Sullivan
1938	T. G. Wilkinson	R. W. Cairns	G. Boswell
1939	A. C. Cunnison	R. W. Cairns	G. Boswell
1940	J. D. Stubbs	R. W. Cairns	No Competition
1941	R. L. Hill	R. W. Cairns	
1942	R. L. Hill	R. W. Cairns	
1943	A. Smith	R. W. Cairns	
1944	A. Smith	R. W. Cairns	
1945	A. Dixon	R. W. Cairns	
1946	W. L. Dann	R. W. Cairns	R. E. Gray
1947	E. J. Corbett	Viscount Ridley	R. E. Gray
1948	E. J. Corbett	Viscount Ridley	R. E. Gray
1949	P. Turton	Viscount Ridley	R. E. Gray
1950	H. L. Smith	Viscount Ridley	H. W. Hindmarsh
1951	R. E. Gray	Viscount Ridley	H. W. Hindmarsh
1952	E. Elsbury	T. R. Jackson	K. Fish
1953	P. Richardson	T. R. Jackson	H. W. Hindmarsh
1954	P. E. Nicholson	T. R. Jackson	D. Moffat
1955	S. H. Partridge	P. Turton	R. E. Gray
1956	A. R. Forsyth	P. Turton	R. E. Gray
1957	C. P. Barton	P. Turton	D. Moffat
1958	T. S. Meikle	R. L. Hill	D. Moffat
1959	J. H. Ferris	R. L. Hill	J. F. Duncan
1960	J. H. Ferris	P. E. Nicholson	R. E. Gray (Cup presented by J. T. Shevill)
1961	T. E. Bramwell	P. E. Nicholson	G. C. Wilkinson
1962	T. R. Percy	C. P. Barton	G. D. Wilkinson
1963 (Altered Course)	F. G. Heads	C. P. Barton	G. Gill
1964	K. Fish	C. P. Barton	G. C. Wilkinson
1965	G. M. Jones	C. P. Barton	G. C. Wilkinson
1966	P. A. Brown	C. P. Barton	D. Moffat
1967	J. H. Thompson	C. P. Barton	A. W. Smith
1968	E. S. Rowlands	A. T. Rutherford	G. C. Wilkinson
1969	W. H. Brooman	A. T. Rutherford	A. S. Roberts

YEAR	CAPTAIN	PRESIDENT	CLUB CHAMPION
1970	J. Browning	T. R. Percy	R. McKenzie
1971	N. F. Finkle	T. R. Percy	R. P. Andrews
1972	G. Elliott	T. R. Percy	D. Moffat
1973	W. A. Balfour	T. A. S. Meikle	S. Elliott
1974	B. Bigley	T. A. S. Meikle	S. Elliott
1975	A. C. Hill	T. A. S. Meikle	S. Elliott
1976	D. Allan	J. Thompson	S. Elliott
1977	J. I. Sleight	P. A. Brown	D. Moffat
1978	R. Mountford	P. A. Brown	R. I. Sleight
1979	J. M. Slater	P. A. Brown	S. H. Reid
1980	H. A. Smith	G. M. Jones	C. W. A'Court
1981	J. A. Taylor	G. M. Jones	J. McGee
1982	B. L. Goldwater	G. H. Thompson	D. Moffat
1983	G. E. Mason	G. H. Thompson	P. Taylor
1984	M. A. Wilkes	J. A. Taylor	D. McCardle
1985	J. F. Duncan	J. A. Taylor	A. M. Harrison
1986	W. R. McAndrew	K. Fish	A. M. Harrison
1987	H. N. Atkinson	K. Fish	D. Moffat
1988	W. Smith	M. C. Beck	M. Blackburn
1989	J. Cairns	M. C. Beck	M. Blackburn
1990	N. B. Dodds	M. C. Beck	A. M. Harrison
1991	J. Spencer	B. L. Goldwater	Not played at time
1992	M. C. Beck	B. L. Goldwater	of going to Press

The City of Newcastle G.C. Clubhouse as it looks today, affording a fine view of the 18th green and fairway.